Dennis J. Cahill

How Consumers Pick a Hotel
Strategic Segmentation and Target Marketing

Pre-publication
REVIEWS,
COMMENTARIES,
EVALUATIONS . . .

More pre-publication
REVIEWS, COMMENTARIES, EVALUATIONS . . .

"**D**espite its provocative title, this new book by Dennis J. Cahill is a serious review of many aspects of market segmentation and strategic design. Mr. Cahill uses the real consumer dilemma of selecting a hotel as a paradigm of consumer choice. He then discusses various theories describing how consumers make such decisions and what marketers can learn from this to improve their strategies. The discussion includes reviews of product positioning and new product introduction. Although not limited exclusively to services, virtually every example is drawn from the service industries, making this a good addition to the services literature.

The core of the book is a lengthy discussion of market segmentation (consumer and industrial) and of the use managers can make of this approach. The specific examples drawn from Mr. Cahill's own experience describe attempts in the real estate industry to segment the housing market using VALS and other similar techniques. The problems and successes of these efforts should be of interest both to managers seeking to learn more about how to use segmentation for their businesses and to academic researchers who would like to know more about what happens in 'real world' service businesses when these efforts are made.

The book abounds with tables and figures that illustrate many of the main points. It is clearly written and easy to read. Managers wishing a brief introduction to the topics covered would find it a good guide to both classic and recent publications on the various topics, betraying Mr. Cahill's wide reading and aptitude at summarizing and integrating large amounts of material. It concludes with case studies of segmentation and recommendations for using segmentation, perceptual mapping, and improving marketing communications based on segmentation. The text would also make a good supplement to an MBA marketing management or marketing strategy course. It contains good practical examples to work through, and provides a thorough review of the marketing concept, market segmentation, and new product introduction strategies."

Ronald E. Goldsmith, PhD
Professor of Marketing,
College of Business,
Florida State University

The Haworth Press, Inc.

How Consumers Pick a Hotel
Strategic Segmentation and Target Marketing

HAWORTH Marketing Resources
Innovations in Practice & Professional Services
William J. Winston, Senior Editor

New, Recent, and Forthcoming Titles:

Church and Ministry Strategic Planning: From Concept to Success by R. Henry Migliore, Robert E. Stevens, and David L. Loudon

Business in Mexico: Managerial Behavior, Protocol, and Etiquette by Candace Bancroft McKinniss and Arthur A. Natella

Managed Service Restructuring in Health Care: A Strategic Approach in a Competitive Environment by Robert L. Goldman and Sanjib K. Mukherjee

A Marketing Approach to Physician Recruitment by James Hacker, Don C. Dodson, and M. Thane Forthman

Marketing for CPAs, Accountants, and Tax Professionals edited by William J. Winston

Strategic Planning for Not-for-Profit Organizations by R. Henry Migliore, Robert E. Stevens, and David L. Loudon

Marketing Planning in a Total Quality Environment by Robert E. Linneman and John L. Stanton, Jr.

Managing Sales Professionals: The Reality of Profitability by Joseph P. Vaccaro

Squeezing a New Service into a Crowded Market by Dennis J. Cahill

Publicity for Mental Health Clinicians: Using TV, Radio, and Print Media to Enhance Your Public Image by Douglas H. Ruben

Managing a Public Relations Firm for Growth and Profit by A. C. Croft

Utilizing the Strategic Marketing Organization: The Modernization of the Marketing Mindset by Joseph P. Stanco

Internal Marketing: Your Company's Next Stage of Growth by Dennis J. Cahill

The Clinician's Guide to Managed Behavioral Care by Norman Winegar

Marketing Health Care into the Twenty-First Century: The Changing Dynamic by Alan K. Vitberg

Fundamentals of Strategic Planning for Health-Care Organizations edited by Stan Williamson, Robert Stevens, David Loudon, and R. Henry Migliore

Risky Business: Managing Violence in the Workplace by Lynne Falkin McClure

Predicting Successful Hospital Mergers and Acquisitions: A Financial and Marketing Analytical Tool by David P. Angrisani and Robert L. Goldman

Marketing Research That Pays Off: Case Histories of Marketing Research Leading to Success in the Marketplace edited by Larry Percy

How Consumers Pick a Hotel: Strategic Segmentation and Target Marketing by Dennis Cahill

Applying Telecommunications and Technology from a Global Business Perspective by Jay Zajas and Olive Church

Strategic Planning for Private Higher Education by Carle M. Hunt, Kenneth W. Oosting, Robert Stevens, David Loudon, and R. Henry Migliore

Writing for Money in Mental Health by Douglas H. Ruben

How Consumers
Pick a Hotel
Strategic Segmentation
and Target Marketing

Dennis J. Cahill

The Haworth Press
New York • London

. The Haworth Press, Inc., 10 Alice Street, Binghamton, NY 13904-1580

Cover design by Donna M. Brooks.

Library of Congress Cataloging-in-Publication Data

Cahill, Dennis J.
   Strategic segmentation and target marketing : how to pick a hotel / Dennis J. Cahill.
      p. cm.
   Includes bibliographical references and index.
   ISBN 0-7890-0184-5 (alk. paper)
    1. Hotels–Marketing. 2. Market segmentation. I. Title.
TX911.3.M3C34 1997
647.94′068′8–dc20

                                         96-41430
                                          CIP

To my wife
Jeanine Gail Zak Cahill
who originated the metaphor that made this book possible

ABOUT THE AUTHOR

Dennis J. Cahill, MBA, MA, has headed North Union Associates, Inc., a finance, investment, and marketing consulting firm in Cleveland, Ohio, since 1983. He founded the firm after almost a decade of increasingly responsible financial positions held in the cement and banking industries. Mr. Cahill has also taught undergraduate and graduate marketing and finance courses at three Cleveland area colleges. The author of *Squeezing a New Service into a Crowded Market* and *Internal Marketing: Your Company's Next Stage of Growth*, he has published numerous articles in scholarly and professional publications and has spoken at national professional conferences and local meetings. In October, 1992, he was appointed editor of the *Journal of Product and Brand Management*. While heading North Union Associates, Mr. Cahill has been active in many aspects of new product and new service development, from initial concept through delivery of completed product to end user. He is a member of the American Marketing Association, the Academy of Management, the Association of Psychological Type, the Association for Consumer Research, the Cleveland Business Economists Club, and The Barnard Society, USA.

CONTENTS

APPENDIX: CASE APPLICATIONS OF SEGMENTATION

Preface

This is Opus 3—my third book for Haworth. This fact would come as a great shock to my eleventh grade English teacher if she knew. She always said that writing a letter seemed beyond my capabilities, as did my eleventh grade American History teacher, and some teachers in college and graduate school. However, this opinion was not shared by my twelfth grade English teacher nor my business school professors.

This book has been a joy to write. As you will read in Chapter 1, the organizing concept came to me in a conversation with my wife, to whom I have gratefully dedicated the book. Six weeks from outline to the end of the first draft is fast, even for me. My kids want me to write a best-seller about the Civil War, not "boring marketing books"—but this one should be anything but boring. The concept of actually implementing a marketing strategy that is well-known and discussed in every marketing textbook should excite you, the reader. The chance is so rarely given us, whatever our field of endeavor.

A road map of the book is in order. Chapter 1 consists of a quick overview of consumer behavior, which is the foundation of all segmentation schemes—or should be. Chapter 2 is a discussion of strategy, target marketing, and why one should segment. Part II consists of three chapters specifically on segmentation—one each on segmentation based on physical attributes, segmentation based on behavioral attributes, and business-to-business segmentation. Part III consists of three chapters on implementation issues. The book concludes with three cases in which clients have actually taken segmentation schemes and sought to apply them in various ways and for various purposes in their day-to-day business—usually successfully, but sometimes with difficulty.

I have the usual author's debts to library personnel, journal editors and anonymous reviewers, friends, and colleagues. In addition, I have debts to clients for giving me interesting consulting engagements and the ability to write about them, and to the people in the VALS (Values and Lifestyle Segmentation) program at Stanford Research Institute for the ability to see VALS in operation over a period of many months–a journey not granted to many in the field. I also have debts to the people at The Haworth Press who took an author with no books to his credit, encouraged him to write his first two books, and then asked for two more–before the first book could have sold more than a dozen copies or been widely reviewed. This is big-league trust. The people I have worked with–from Bill Winston, my editor, to all of the people in Binghamton, especially Peg Marr and Dawn Krisko, production editors for *Squeezing a New Service into a Crowded Market* and *Internal Marketing: Your Company's Next Stage of Growth*, have been uniformly easy to work with and have been understanding about the birthing process that a book represents to the author.

And I owe a debt to you, the reader. This book is intended to be read and *used* by practitioners and students alike. It has pages of marketing theory interlaced with stories of how to implement the theory. I hope it works for you. Let me know.

PART I:
GETTING READY

Chapter 1

"How Do You Pick a Hotel?":
A Brief Look at Consumer Behavior

To serve as an introduction to the subject of target marketing and segmentation, I would like to look at the subject of consumer choice from the consumer's viewpoint for a moment, as we will be spending most of the book looking at choice from the producer's viewpoint. The choice of organizing metaphor occurred during a recent family trip to Florida, coming soon after a similar trip to Oregon. In neither case did I make the hotel selection—but let us begin.

In 1995, my parents lived in Eugene, Oregon, a town of approximately 125,000, located in central Oregon. The town has two industries: lumber products and the University of Oregon. Eugene sports several hotels and motels: at the time, a downtown Hilton, a Holiday Inn, and a Red Lion led the list of "big names." Near the University there is a plethora of cheap motels of no distinction, plus a few where visiting faculty and parents feel comfortable staying. The leading motel in town is the Valley River Inn, a large facility away from the University on the Willamette River near Valley River Center shopping mall. Containing well over 200 rooms, it boasts meeting facilities and a good restaurant. My family had stayed there before while visiting my parents and we were quite satisfied with it.

When it came time to plan our stay for the fall 1995 trip to Eugene, my parents suggested the Holiday Inn; it was closer to their house, the kids would stay and eat free, there was a playground at the motel, and the room rate was considerably less. I told my kids that Grandma wanted them to stay at the Holiday Inn instead of the Valley River; they were vocally disappointed. I told them that Grandma and Grandpa were paying for the hotel and if they wanted to dispute their grandparents' choice, they had better do it because I was going to stay out of the fight. Needless to say, grandparents being what they are, we stayed at the Valley River Inn.

Why? There is nothing wrong with Holiday Inns. My kids don't know that, having never stayed in one before; although my daughter has stayed in one (but not my son), it was so long ago that she does not remember. But they had stayed in the Valley River Inn and wanted to go back there, preferably to the same room.

Why the loyalty? For one thing, there is the inertia endemic to children—the comfort of doing something again versus the discomfort of doing something for the first time. But there is more. The Valley River Inn staff work hard to make their guests feel welcomed, whether they were five and nine, or fifty-nine. Further, there were touches that would stick in any customer's mind. The Valley River's turndown service features a large Red Delicious apple on the pillow rather than a mint—this *is* Oregon, after all. They rent bicycles to their guests to ride along the bike path that runs for miles along the river right outside the hotel. Wild blackberry bushes abound right outside the hotel grounds, free for the picking and eating with breakfast. All in all, I cannot quibble with my kids' choice of hotels.

Then, in November, we took another trip, this time to Daytona Beach where my in-laws have a second home. My father-in-law made the reservations for us; his first choice was the Days Inn (because they had stayed there while looking for their mobile home and were familiar with it), but the inn did not have any rooms, so we stayed at the Ramada Inn Surfside. It was a satisfactory hotel, with a full kitchen so that we could eat breakfast in the room, and the usual beach hotel amenities—pool, beach, pool towels, etc. Nothing great, but more than adequate.

With a population in the area of a quarter of a million, there are an astounding number of hotels and motels on the beach. The Daytona Beach (and area) Yellow Pages lists thirteen pages of hotels and twenty-seven pages of motels. Even allowing for some duplications between the categories, this is an awful lot of guest rooms. By contrast, the Cleveland Yellow Pages directory has four pages for an area not only seven times larger in population, but larger in geographical extent. But Daytona, of course, is a snowbird destination and needs hundreds of hotels to house them.

And what a variety of properties! Everything from an Adam's Mark hotel across from the new convention center to an eight-room concrete-block building right out of the 1950's matchbook cover. "You can own your own business." In the approximate mile between our hotel and my in-laws' mobile home, there was a large Comfort Inn, a Holiday Inn (which my kids booed every time we passed, in memory of my parents' attempt to deny them staying at the Valley River Inn), a Days Inn, a Howard Johnson's, fifteen smaller motels, at least two "beach club" time-shares, two large condominiums (with rooms for rent, certainly during the out-of-season period) with another huge condo building going up. On the ocean side of the street, there is nothing but rooms for rent. Everything else—bathing suit and souvenir shops, miniature golf, ABC stores, restaurants, shopping centers—is on the other side of Route A1A, as are a few motels.

How does one make a decision about where to stay? When I asked my father-in-law why he had picked the Ramada when the Days Inn was full, he said: "Easy. It was the only name we could remember in Cleveland when we made the reservation." This, of course, is a clear statement of the need for advertising and the biggest signs allowable so that people will remember your property. But how is someone supposed to decide from a Yellow Pages entry? Do you stay at Holiday Inn (no surprises)? Not in my family anymore. Treasure Island Inn? Turtle Inn (a clear favorite with my kids because of the name and the sign outside)? Anchorage Family Motel (with its unmistakable Alaskan overtones)? Buccaneer Motel? Caravel Motel? Lazy Hours Motel? New Frontier Motel (with its two heated pools)? Peter Pan Motel (on the "wrong" side of the A1A)? Robin Hood Motel? The Talisman? Or the Whale Watch Motel? How does one choose?

Obviously, the Yellow Pages are not the only source for information that a typical traveler will use. There are the AAA Guides, and others, which give facts and figures —and sometimes great descriptions. After one has visited an area once, other possible hotels or motels seem to jump out. When we stayed in Newport, Oregon, we chose the Whaler Inn from the AAA Guide based on the description and the name, and were not disappointed. When we drove around the area, we noticed a bed-and-breakfast guest house that would be nice if we returned after our kids were old enough to stay at a bed-and-breakfast. But how does a customer choose?

A large amount of research and writing has gone into the field of consumer psychology and behavior over the years. Much of this research has led to the development of various models of consumer behavior, both graphic and mathematical. Two of the earliest and most prominent models, at least one of which will be familiar to all who have had a course in consumer behavior in the last twenty years or who read the chapter on consumer behavior (or, if they are old enough, the chapter on "buyer behavior") in their general marketing textbook are: the Howard-Sheth model (see Figure 1.1) and the Engel-Kollat-Blackwell (EKB) model (see Figure 1.2). Both are elaborated on in Engel and Blackwell (1982) and other textbooks. These models attempt to describe and explain the process by which consumers decide to buy a product or service. As they are presented, they seem terribly overelaborate; often it seems that consumers conduct the entire process in an unconscious state.

Although I would not wish to diminish the differences between the two models, there are remarkable similarities. Both start with the recognition by the consumer that there is a dichotomy between a desired state and reality, proceed through a process of searching for a way to end the dichotomy, weighing alternatives, making a choice, making the actual purchase (thus betraying the "buyer-behavior" orientation of the field in the 1960s and 1970s), and dealing with the outcome. Although these models probably do not describe the process by which we buy chewing gum or other trivial items, they probably do fit, at least in descriptive terms, the way we buy houses and cars. (See Cahill, 1994a for an extension to this model for houses.)

How do the models deal with the choice of a hotel? Let's follow through the steps in the unelaborated EKB model (Figure 1.3) and see. We start with "Problem Recognition." My family was going to visit grandparents, neither of whom had enough room for the four of us in their house; therefore, we needed a room to rent. The next step is "Search." In neither case above was "Search" particularly elaborate; there were not that many alternatives in Eugene to choose from, and in Daytona Beach, although there are hundreds of alternatives, my in-laws could not remember any of them. "Alternative

FIGURE 1.1. Howard-Sheth Consumer-Behavior Model

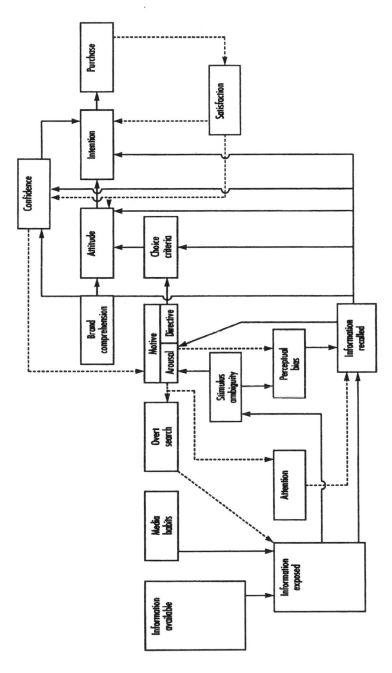

Source: Adapted from Engel and Blackwell (1982), p. 680.

7

FIGURE 1.2. Engel and Blackwell Consumer-Behavior Model

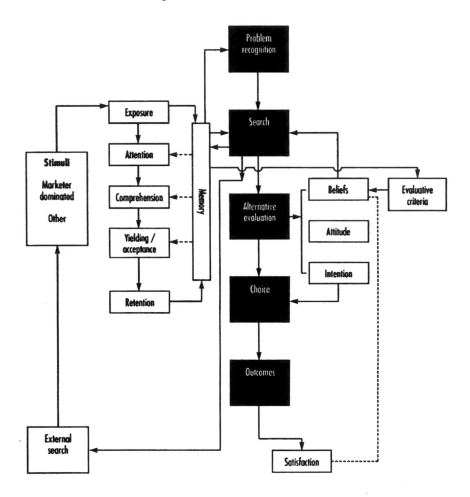

Source: Adapted from Engel and Blackwell (1982), p. 33.

evaluation" was simplicity itself in Daytona Beach: Days Inn had no rooms, Ramada Inn did, and that was it. In Eugene, however, none of the alternatives truly mattered because of a behavioral idio-syncrasy in the buying unit, in this case, the grandparents. "Choice" is almost a misnomer in both cases because there were no choices to be made. "Outcome" was favorable in both cases. Is the model descriptive of the process? It appears to be–at least in these cases.

However, in the almost-thirty years since the EKB model was developed, there has been a shift in the field of consumer behavior studies. As mentioned above, the field used to be focused on "buyer behavior," but that has changed; the same tools have been used on actions where no money changes hands, such as the viewing of television shows, with gratifying results. Holt has developed a

FIGURE 1.3. Simplified Engel and Blackwell Consumer-Behavior Model

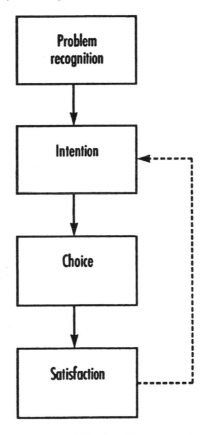

Source: Adapted from Engel and Blackwell (1982), p. 34.

typology of how consumers consume and what types of actions are subsumed in the term "consume" (1995). Although most consumer studies have traditionally been psychology-based, there have been some attempts to look at the social and societal components (Nicosia and Mayer, 1976; Hirschman, 1985; Rook, 1985).

In perhaps the most sweeping and drastic argument about consumer behavior, Morris Holbrook issued a call to change the entire field of consumer research away from buying and back to consuming, saying:

> I . . . propose an expansion of consumer research to reflect a fuller treatment of (1) consuming (versus buying), (2) experiencing (versus deciding), (3) using products (versus choosing brands), (4) intangible services and ideas (versus tangible goods), (5) more (versus fewer) durable products, (6) expenditures of time, effort, and ability (versus money), (7) emotional components (versus narrowly defined affect), (8) consumer misbehavior (versus behavior), (9) mutually interdependent wholes (versus their parts), and (10) concern with consumption for its own sake (versus managerial relevance). . . . (1987:173)

In the years since Holbrook's call, much of this has happened; some had happened before it. The study of consumers and consumption is now close to being truly multidisciplinary; we are examining aspects of the process that were never thought important before. In fact, Holbrook's *Consumer Research* (1995) captures the history of change in detail. (See also Cahill, 1996b and 1996c for a review of the field, and Cahill, 1994b for a brief discussion of some of the problems such a stance creates.)

Nevertheless, there is one part of Holbrook's call that is disturbing: there runs through the entire book in which the Holbrook chapter appears a sense that consumer research should be elevated to the status of "consumer science" and divorced from any taint of usefulness; much of this plaint seems to derive from the fact that most of the consumer researchers are housed in business schools and thus lack academic respectability—certainly in the eyes of many of their colleagues in arts and sciences. As a former graduate student in American history, I can understand, empathize, and sympathize with those who desire to do research that interests them, regardless of whether it leads to anything "useful," as Holbrook so adamantly hopes for. However, there is a question of the worth of much of what passes for "research" in the consumer field; it frequently seems to have been designed to avoid any taint of usefulness. And worse, all too often when one reads the published results of much of it, one has a sense of "so what?" I can cite dozens of examples, but will refrain. Rather, I will cite some conditions which should serve as red flags to the problem when one reads such a research paper, although the presence of one of these conditions should not be read as disabling—nor even two or three, necessarily.

First, the paper is based on the author's dissertation. Second, a sample of students is utilized. If the research is about computer programs, CDs, jeans, T-shirts, or other items which college students buy and use, such a sample is no problem. However, if the study is about cars, houses, cooking, or something similar—beware. Third, a long list of references having to do with deconstructionism, postmodernism, or some other "in" topic is a sure indication that the author is off doing research that will bear no relationship to anything in the "real world." Fourth, the authors start out with the statement that their qualitative methodology needs to be considered "science" and cite Thomas Kuhn's 1970 seminal work; as I have complained elsewhere, this is a waste of talent (Cahill, 1993). Again, I am not stating that all research needs to be applications-oriented; my point is that too much of what is being done in consumer research is simply incestuous, academic mental masturbation, designed to build a curriculum *vita* for the author so that when it is time to build a tenure file, the requisite number of publications in the "right" journals will be there. It certainly does not create answers to questions that anyone outside of academe has ever asked. Rather, if one wants answers to the questions normally asked by practitioners—what do people want? how much do they want? what will they pay?—one needs to go to different sources. *The Wall Street Journal* published two studies in 1990 which answered these questions in no uncertain terms (1990a, 1990b), but they certainly need updating by now.

It is my contention here, and that contention will be reinforced throughout the remainder of the book, that the consumer's choice is led by the producing firm which has targeted a particular kind of customer that it wants. It does this through a variety of methods:

from the name it chooses and the logo it designs, to the methods by which it communicates with its customers. And, of course, by the content of those communications. Ramada has recently advertised to the travel industry that they are changing, stating, "We are simplifying our choice of properties–making it easier for your clients to pinpoint the type of Ramada they'll need on any given trip." Pollay and Mittal (1993) have even used segmentation by personal utility and socioeconomic factors to identify attitudinal segments toward advertising in general in the U.S. population.

A successful firm will be conscious of the targeting and communications, integrating these into a coherent, consistent message which is conveyed to the customers and prospects. An unsuccessful or less successful firm will not have a tight grasp on the program, and its messages will be scrambled. Keeping with the hotel and motel example used here, a name such as Robin Hood would be used, not for a "quaint," family-friendly motel, but for an establishment that seeks business travelers. The clerk at the Ramada Surfside commented that I made a lot of phone calls (eight in a week); any hotel that specialized in business travelers might have asked instead if the telephone in my room had been broken!

How does a firm decide which customers it should target? That is the subject of the next chapter.

Chapter 2

Strategic Planning and Implications

In their book on strategy, Hamel and Prahalad (1994) claim that there are "three kinds of companies: companies that try to lead customers where they don't want to go (these are companies that find the idea of being customer-led an insight); companies that listen to customers and then respond to their articulated needs (needs that are probably already being satisfied by more foresightful competitors); and companies that lead customers where they want to go, but don't know it yet. Companies that create the future do more than satisfy customers, they constantly amaze them" (1994:100). Both of the first two kinds of companies can benefit from an application of target marketing; the third is undoubtedly already practicing target marketing.

Strategic planning is, to Hamel and Prahalad, a "feasibility sieve." It is a tool for ensuring that questions of practicality are answered. Strategic planning in this sense is used to reject goals and objectives when the means of obtaining them are not at hand. Although Hamel and Prahalad mean this to be an indictment of planning, I disagree that it is such. They state that "when what is feasible drives out what is desirable, an ambitious strategic intent becomes impossible. . ." (Hamel and Prahalad, 1994:145). However, if the most desirable of goals is beyond the reach of a firm, is it worth striving for? Great strategic planning, rather, is the matching of feasibility with ambition. Although Figure 2.1, a simple-looking 2×2 matrix, purports to show where the firm should be going (Quadrant I in the upper right-hand corner), I feel either of the right-hand quadrants will do. If the firm has adequate resources to attain Quadrant I, fine; otherwise, serving Quadrant IV by understanding the articulated wants and needs of that market better than

FIGURE 2.1. Where Should the Firm Be Going?

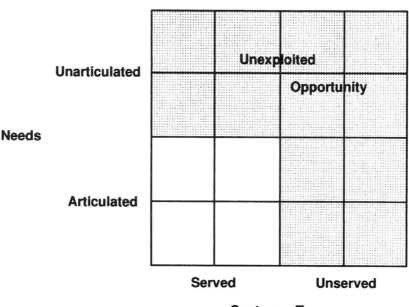

Source: Adapted from Hamel and Prahalad (1994), p. 103.

other firms will allow the firm to obtain better-than-average results with limited resources. If the firm has relatively unlimited resources, Quadrant I certainly is better.

And this is part of the challenge of a segmentation strategy: the goal of allocating resources more efficiently and more effectively must be balanced against the cost of developing and administering a number of marketing programs from product development of (potentially) numerous iterations of (possibly) similar products to the communicating of these differences to different segments (Neidell, 1983). At the level of defining the business, it is sometimes possible to segment very simply. For example, Snap-On Tool Corporation states in its definition of who Snap-On Tool is that they will sell tools to professional mechanics (Day, 1984). Although it would be possible to further segment the automotive tool market (and

Snap-On may do so), this is a first cut through the possible customers for automotive tools.

Remember what the goal is here: to gain competitive advantage. As Porter pompously puts it, the crucial strategic questions here are: where in an industry to compete and which segments to focus on for sustainable advantage (Porter, 1985). Porter's focus is outward; he wants a firm to find segments that match its capabilities rather than building capabilities that match customer needs. This is a clear violation of the Marketing Concept, which will be discussed below. And if Ralph Stacey (1992) is correct, that bounded instability describes the current (and certainly the future) state of business, it will be difficult in the years ahead to find sustainable competitive advantage by looking for segments which meet our current capabilities.

How does segmentation lead to competitive advantage for a firm? It reduces rivalry because there should be fewer competitors in any given segment; this should reduce downward pricing pressures. It reduces pressure from substitutes, because certain segments will not see a rival product as a substitute (Schnaars, 1991). Further, it allows a firm to become the product of choice in a segment, even if the firm is relatively small. Also, the firm can become the recognized expert on a segment, which may pay dividends for years in terms of lower product development costs.

In short, segmentation creates barriers to entry into the market that are not related to any potential antitrust problems. These barriers are investment levels needed to play on the field with the rest of the teams; they represent investment in plant and equipment, certainly, but also (and more important) experience. I have a client who has developed a computer program that writes classified advertisements for residential real estate (more about this client and its products later). The research into this program now stretches back twenty years; although the computer program could probably be duplicated without excessive difficulty, anyone wishing to sell a similar program will start at a disadvantage because they lack the twenty-year investment in learning about the real estate industry, what makes a good real-estate advertisement, what buyers want in houses and ads, what agents want, and so forth. As Davidow (1986) expresses it, segmenting and building a segment into a true target, developing not market share but share of the market in the segment, allows a small firm to own a segment, allows a David to slay a Goliath. It is competitive advantage in spades!

TARGET MARKETING DEFINED AND EXPLAINED

Not all customers are alike. As unprofound as this statement may appear, it is one that needs to be repeated frequently. Hallberg makes the point succinctly by making it the title of his book (1995). He further makes the point bluntly in stating that the Pareto Principle holds–and the 20 percent (or whatever the percentage actually is) who are your most profitable customers are going to be the only group that holds your brand's profits above water in the future. Further, if you do not build brand loyalty through a sound loyalty program with your high-profit customers, you are dead. Duboff (1992) phrases this a bit differently, stating that the steps are to identify *profitable* customers, learn their values, analyze the offerings they need and use, focus marketing on them (and, implicitly, ignore the nonprofitable customers), and monitor their satisfaction. This is as good and succinct a description of target marketing and segmentation for profitability as I have seen.

A "Target Market" is, at its most basic, simply the market or submarket (such as a segment) at which the firm aims its marketing message(s). There is nothing inherent in the concept of target marketing that requires a firm to segment, or–having segmented–to develop multiple product offerings or marketing messages. It simply means that a group of customers has been identified for whom the offering should be "right" and to whom the firm will direct the majority of its marketing time, resources, and attention, with the rationale that it is better to use a rifle than a shotgun to get results. (This rationale possibly should be reconsidered; in the Gunfight at OK Corral, it was Doc Holliday using a shotgun who killed people, not the Earps using pistols.) Nevertheless, it seems usual that when firms target market, they do so for multiple targets within a broader market.

In a brief case study, Freeman (1992) outlines the story of COMBAT, an insecticide which followed a highly targeted strategy with a degree of success. But as Freeman points out, there are problems with such a strategy. "The only disadvantage of this focused segmentation approach was that while the business was clearly stronger where advertising was focused, it was also clearly less strong where it was not focused" (Freeman, 1992:17). Provided sales in the target segment are higher than lost sales in the nontarget, the firm is undoubtedly better off financially. Even if it is a wash, I would stipulate that the firm is better off because it has focused its time and effort instead of spreading the resources around. Al Ries (1992) agrees, stating that the discipline of a narrow focus is important in building a viable strategy.

Anything new in the above? Not really, at least not for those who have kept up with trends in several areas of marketing, namely database and direct marketing. The major thrust of the Hallberg thesis, however, is that all of this applies to branded packaged goods; one of the examples he cites over and over again is Ziploc bags—hardly a big-ticket item. Much of what he says has been touted for years for higher-priced items; Hallberg states that the same points are true for a grocery store item costing about $1.00 per unit, or even less.

Hallberg, who has worked at both J. Walter Thompson and (currently) Ogilvy and Mather, reports on several years of research done by task forces at Ogilvy which investigated the erosion of margins at their clients; the cause was increased spending on promotion and reduced spending on advertising—nothing new here, either. Nor without self-interest, as advertising agencies typically make higher fees from advertising than promotion. The leap that Hallberg was able to make was to translate this statement into a means of building brand profitability by building customer loyalty to the brand. He states that loyal customers will spend more for the brands in their considered set. When this is coupled with a search for the heavy users in the category (again, hardly a new concept), the willingness to pay a higher price plus heavier-than-average usage of the product makes for explosive profitability of this segment. And Hallberg presents the mathematics to back up his assertions. It is clear (and intuitive) that loyal heavy users make a bigger-than-average contribution to the brand's profitability. The difficulty is in finding these people and keeping them loyal; but there is no doubt that such a search is worthwhile.

That is what target marketing is all about: defining who we want to attract–and striving to ensure these individuals will be the loyal, high-profit customers that Hallberg and others emphasize. And, at least as important, defining who it is that we do not care to attract. Target marketing implies that there are customers whom we do not wish to target, that we will serve if possible but will make no special effort to serve–and that there may be individuals whom we do not wish to serve at all. And that is all that a target market consists of–and truly all that target marketing is.

This is also called "positioning"–which focuses on the product or service offering rather than on the customer who will buy and use the product or service (and gives exactly the wrong focus to an organization). Brooksbank (1994) states that developing the positioning strategy is time consuming and difficult; it requires one to build up a picture of the marketplace and how one is going to compete (and with whom). It is a painful process for any organization to undergo.

Then why is target marketing so important? There are really two major reasons. The first is that it forces a strategic focus to the firm, forcing the firm to look toward a realistic approach to its customers and its product/service offerings and to determine the best fit(s) between them. Second, it forces a strategic focus on the firm that begins outside with the customers, the market, and not inside with the firm. In short, it requires the use of the Marketing Concept as part of the firm's strategic marketing planning.

THE MARKETING CONCEPT

The Marketing Concept is not new. It is now forty years since John McKitterick (1957) put forth the idea that the Marketing Concept is a customer-oriented, integrated, profit-oriented philosophy of business. In the ensuing years, while there has been profound debate on the idea (e.g., Hirschman, 1983), the concept has survived. An undergraduate marketing text taken at random from my bookshelves devotes two pages of explanation and a chart to the Marketing Concept explaining–with little change from McKitterick–that it is a "customer-oriented, integrated, goal-oriented philosophy for a firm, institution, or person" (Evans and Berman, 1987:12-14).

One would expect that any concept so basic as to appear in an introductory textbook would be wholeheartedly subscribed to by practitioners and academics alike. In the case of the Marketing Concept, however, nothing could be further from the truth. Again, to sample my files at random, Hirschman (1983:45) proposes that the concept is not applicable to artists and ideologists because of "the personal values and social norms that characterize the production process" of these persons' output. Berry (1988:28), in an article aimed at practitioners, states that the Marketing Concept "will continue to gain in importance and application." Hampton and Lane (1982) state that the marketing concept is anathema to at least a large portion of the employees in the newspaper industry on the editorial side. John C. Crawford (1983:450) states that the Marketing Concept "appears to be an impossible philosophy to put into effect. . . . [It] is still loudly proclaimed but seldom seen. It represents the unattainable—the marketing utopia."

I have often written to defend the Marketing Concept. Cahill (1992b and 1992c) take a relatively lighthearted and untraditional look at ways to organize successful marketing efforts around the concept. Cahill (1992a and 1996a) look at the Marketing Concept as a way to prevent overinnovativenes, to the detriment of client needs in professional-service firms. Cahill and Warshawsky (1993) reiterate the importance of the concept even in high-technology products, stating that these types of products are not exempt from the workings of consumer behavior that drives the Marketing Concept, despite the feelings of all too many people that high tech is immune from these considerations. Cahill, Warshawsky, and Thach (1994) similarly reiterate this fact, using the fate of two computer software programs as case studies. Thus, with this background of thought and writing on the subject of the Marketing Concept (rather extensive and on a somewhat philosophical topic for a nonacademic), I am hardly "objective" on the subject, much less dispassionate. I strongly believe that the Marketing Concept, properly understood and correctly implemented, is one of the basic tools in the marketer's tool kit, and it seems to me that it provides a good starting point to any consideration of marketing strategy. When one combines the Marketing Concept with the realization that not all customers are alike, one has a powerful tool.

Remembering that the Marketing Concept starts with the wishes of the customer and that not all customers are alike leads directly to the realization that there must be more than one type of customer for any given service or product. This is the foundation of segmentation as a strategy. One must offer either an array of different products and services to the different groups–if the firm has sufficient resources to do so–or only try to reach the group of customers for whom the firm's single offering will be in line with their wishes.

The current state of "interactive technology" has caught the eye of a few marketing thinkers in the past couple of years. Peppers and Rogers (1993) have posited what they call "one-to-one" marketing, where the vendor will be in direct contact (and vice versa) with each potential buyer, seeking what they call "share of customer" rather than "market share." This viewpoint seems to negate the need to target market for several reasons. First, as Peppers and Rogers–and others who agree with them–say, the customers who are interested in your offerings will seek you out. The Internet and the World Wide Web will allow people with the use of computer search engines to find the firms who have offerings in the categories in which they are interested. Second, segmentation and targeting philosophically exclude certain people for various reasons; the use of one-to-one marketing allows all people to be potential customers. Third, the database developed from marketing electronically to the people who want the firm's offerings will allow those people to self-select into the target market and allow the firm to do what Hallberg wants: focus exclusively on the heavy users of the firm's products and services, for these become the most profitable customers.

This is not the place to go into depth about marketing on the Internet; suffice it to say that the vision enunciated above, while attractive, has a couple of defective premises. First, not enough people are currently hooked up to the Internet, nor do they seem to buy (as opposed to shop) on the Internet. For every success story–such as the widely trumpeted 1-800-FLOWERS–there seem to be many stories which do not get the coverage, of companies who have tried the Internet with minimal success. Second, one still needs to get the message out about one's offerings. Peppers and Rogers, and others who subscribe to their thesis, posit a Golden Age of Mass Marketing, where everyone watched *Leave It to Beaver* and bought

Tide. Given this Golden Age of Mass Marketing, the current media seem inefficient, considering the changes in the population and communications technology. But I was alive during that "Golden Age," never watched *Leave It to Beaver* (we were an NBC family) and my mother *never* bought Tide. Even in this "Golden Age," markets were segmented.

What do we wish to gain strategically by segmenting, beyond the realization that we cannot be all things to all comers and that some customers are not worth having? Competitive advantage. We want to develop customers in the segments that are most profitable to our firm by giving the customers in those segments what they want and communicating with them in language that they can understand. If we can do this in a way that keeps customers that we do not want to attract from seeing or hearing our communications and thus staying away, so much the better. This is what Yavitz and Newman (1982:162) in another context have called "The Right Person and the Right Carrot." In other words, the correct segment of customers and the correct offering. This is the easiest and surest method for developing competitive advantage—doing something better than the competition. One potential source of competitive advantage that has long been a part of strategic and marketing theory is the so-called "pioneer advantage," the advantage in building market share that accrues to the first firm to introduce a product or service.

PIONEER ADVANTAGE

The subject of how the market share leader got to be that way is a venerable research topic in marketing and macroeconomics, and for good reason: market share leadership generally conveys at least the notion of superior profitability for the firm as well as the expectation of continued organizational strength in years to come. Further, the fascination with high-tech products and the purported advantages of being first on the downward-sloping cost curve implied by "experience-curve" benefits so frequently and facilely discussed (based apparently on the economic history of the semiconductor industry) seems to make it imperative to come to market with a new product and capture as big a share as possible as quickly as possible in order to build a position as the lowest-cost producer which will protect the firm from later comers. In fact, a mythology approaching the status of conventional wisdom has built up over the years that durable market share leaders tend to have been, if not the first, then early entrants into their product categories.

That mythology is as prevalent in the academic literature (or possibly more so) as it is in the practitioner literature. Kerin, Varadarajan, and Peterson (1992) have synthesized several previous studies and created seventeen research propositions to test; their conclusion is that the phenomenon of pioneer advantage is more complex than much of the literature suggests. Golder and Tellis (1993) state that almost half of the market pioneers in their sample of 500 brands in fifty product categories failed and the survivors' mean market share is lower than that found in other studies. Further, their study shows that early market leaders (as distinct from first entrants) have much greater long-term success; those in their sample entered an average of thirteen years later than the pioneers. Robinson (1988) studied a cross section of industrial markets and discovered that market pioneers tend to have higher market shares than late entrants, primarily because they have a stronger product in relation to those of their competitors. This is, of course, a cursory look at some recent academic work on the subject and makes no claim to be anything else. Nevertheless, it seems to represent the way that academic marketing researchers have looked at the question for the past several years. And, of course, the reference lists in the above-mentioned articles cite earlier research—back to the late 1970s.

Two works were published in 1994 that brought this research into stark relief. Carpenter and Nakamoto received the 1994 William F. O'Dell Award for their article "Consumer Preference Formation and Pioneering Advantage" (Carpenter and Nakamoto, 1989) and published their reflections on their original article and on what had happened in the intervening years (Carpenter and Nakamoto, 1994). The O'Dell Award is presented annually for the article published in the *Journal of Marketing Research* five years previously that is judged to have made the greatest contribution to marketing research.

To briefly summarize their original article, Carpenter and Nakamoto describe a learning model of preference formation for products that are new; buyers approach new products with "weakly formed" preferences for attributes. They update their preferences through trial and usage of the product. Pioneers earn a competitive advantage through this process in two ways. First, a pioneer develops the best preference position with consumers by shifting the taste distribution toward *its* position and by influencing the attribute weights buyers use to evaluate brands in the category. Second, because the pioneer has a central role in consumers' preference formation in the category, the pioneer becomes the prototype for brands in the category; in terms of high tech, they become the "standard." (Compare this with Robinson's 1988 statement about pioneering industrial marketers having a "stronger" product than their competitors.) It is this second effect that truly protects the pioneer from later entrants. Carpenter and Nakamoto then conducted two experiments to test their model and found that the experiments did, in fact, validate their hypotheses, though subject to various caveats and limitations that are fairly standard and routine in academic research reports.

In their later article, Carpenter and Nakamoto state that their earlier work suggests that consumer preferences are, at least in part, the outcome of competition. "Lacking fixed exogenous preferences, buyers learn their preferences through trial and error"–deciding what attributes they do and do not like on the basis of available alternatives. Their preferences evolve with experience and are not created out of whole cloth. Competition in a new category "can be viewed in part as a race to shape the nature of consumer preferences" and, of course, the early entrants have a head start in that race. *Pioneering advantage, however, is realized only if the first mover succeeds in framing consumer preferences.* If the first mover fails at that task, the field is left open for later entrants. Thus, pioneering advantage is not automatic. It needs to be earned through the execution of competent marketing programs" (Carpenter and Nakamoto, 1994).

The second work published in 1994 is Steven Schnaars's *Managing Imitation Strategies.* The thesis of this book is stated in its subtitle: "How later entrants seize markets from pioneers." The heart of this book–almost 160 pages out of 240–consists of twenty-eight product cases where the pioneer failed to hold a long-term market leadership and was sometimes driven out of the market altogether (and sometimes out of business) by later entrants. Many of the cases are for familiar household products–VCRs and microwave ovens, for example–and five are for various soft drinks and beers. Schnaars carefully builds his case that there is really no such thing as pioneer advantage. He defines pioneer idiosyncratically, but not incorrectly as "any of those firms introducing a product to the market *up to and including* the first to sell it successfully" (Schnaars, 1994:14). He then looks at some of the scholarly research on pioneer advantage. He explores eight articles going back to 1977 which claim to find some and reexamines them in detail, finding that many truly do not point to pioneering advantage for one reason or another. He then looks at five articles that found advantage for later entrants. Schnaars concludes that, given what he considers to be the flawed nature of the studies propounding pioneer advantage–they tend to be theoretical, experimental, or not really looking at new products as the term is usually used–and given the known high costs of innovating as well as the high failure rate of new products, it is probably wiser (and certainly a valid strategy, which is really his main point) to let someone else do the innovating and then jump into the market when its potential is proven and try to wrest market share away from the pioneer.

This is the strategy–sometimes referred to as the "fast second"– which Schnaars claims that Coca-Cola uses to co-opt new products introduced by others, most notably Royal Crown Cola, a persistent but unsuccessful product innovator. However, in view of the fact that the name of the game (even by Schnaars's admission) in soft drinks is distribution and shelf space in stores, and given that Coca-Cola has as many U.S. bottlers as Pepsi and Royal Crown *combined*, can anyone else succeed with a new product? Or, further along these lines, consider IBM's late and watchful introduction of a personal computer in 1981 (and not in really meaningful numbers until 1983); at that time, no other company in the computer industry–even Apple–was truly viewed as "legitimate" by most potential purchasers. This was a product category waiting to happen, waiting for IBM to tell buyers that personal computers were useful products and not toys. In terms of Carpenter and Nakamoto's (1989) formulation, the one product attribute missing from pre-IBM-introduction personal computers was the only part of the PCs which IBM manufactured itself–the blue, three-initial nameplate.

Schnaars then concludes with the three generic strategies which doomed the pioneers in his case studies (see Table 2.1 for the strategies). The only later entrant strategy which can generally be successfully defended against by a pioneer is the "imitate and improve" strategy when the pioneer is willing to continuously improve its own product and not worry about cannibalizing sales by so doing. If the pioneer does not do so, later entrants are handed the opportunity of eating into the pioneer's market. It is clear that pioneer advantage is not permanent and God-given; it is merely a *head start*. Further, because so many new products get stuck in a long, useless stage, pioneers need to have staying power, which can be conferred only by market power or financial and managerial strength from another industry.

Where does this recitation of these two works leave us? At an impasse. Schnaars's work, despite what seem to be some definitional and methodological problems, clearly shows that in some circumstances, later entrants can certainly dominate a market, forcing the pioneer into insignificance in an industry that it started, or even driving it out of business altogether. Carpenter and Nakamoto simply represent the most recent of a long stream of research which has shown that it is *possible* for pioneers to dominate a category for decades. In fact, it would appear that the answer to which of these positions is correct is that it depends. Until a meta-analysis of the research studies is completed, it is difficult to ascertain whether there are any patterns in the apparently contradictory research results. For instance, do consumer products favor the pioneer (one of the classic examples of a pioneer dominating its industry for decades is Wrigley's chewing gum) while industrial goods favor later entrants? Does high tech go one way, low tech another? At this point, we cannot say, yet possible patterns in the results may be important to know.

But, important as is this strategic question of whether to be a pioneer or late entrant, it is an inappropriate question to ask in a *marketing* context. The question that both sides ask is "Should I innovate or imitate in my new product development efforts?" This is a strategic question, a board-of-directors question. Will Coca-Cola innovate or imitate? Will IBM? The *marketing* question is one of the following. First, "the folks in the lab came up with this new

TABLE 2.1. How Imitators Surpassed Pioneers

Product	Lower Prices	Imitate and Improve	Market Power
1. 35mm cameras	X	X	
2. Automated tellers			X
3. Ballpoint pens	X	X	
4. Caffeine-free drinks			X
5. CAT scanners		X	X
6. Commercial jets		X	
7. Computerized ticketing		X	
8. Credit/charge cards			X
9. Diet soft drinks			X
10. Dry beer			X
11. Food processors	X		
12. Light beer			X
13. Mainframe computers			X
14. Microwave ovens	X		
15. Money-market funds			X
16. MRIs	X		X
17. Nonalcoholic beer			X
18. PC operating systems		X	X
19. Paperback books			X
20. Personal computers	X		
21. Pocket calculators	X		
22. Projection television	X	X	X
23. Spreadsheet programs		X	
24. Answering machines	X		X
25. VCRs	X	X	
26. Video games		X	
27. Warehouse clubs			X
28. Word processing software		X	

Source: Schnaars (1994), p. 212.

product. How do we create a defensible pioneering advantage?" Or else, "Our competitors came out with an innovation. How do we copy it and gain market share to shove them out of first place?" Fortunately, both Carpenter and Nakamoto and Schnaars give practical, useable methods to accomplish these tasks and move us along from the apparent impasse.

Pioneer Defense

The best defense for a pioneer is to keep innovating, to continue to improve the product itself in order to leave as little room in the market as possible for later entrants. This boils down to *not* getting stuck at one end of the price spectrum as Xerox and Cuisinart did so disastrously, ceding the low end of the spectrum to others because of low profit margins on the products given their cost accounting systems. This practice allows a later entrant to take the low end (perhaps buying market share at the expense of shorter-term profitability) and greatly expand the size of the market as they drop the price, trapping the pioneer in a small niche at the upper end of the price range. Later buyers are frequently quite different from early buyers in their wants and values and feature-set preferences; desk-top copiers do not truly compete with Xerox's behemoths, nor did the small, inexpensive food processors compete on feature-sets with Cuisinart's models. But the best defense for a pioneer seems to be to continue to improve the product, cannibalizing from its own pioneer products and not allowing a later entrant to take the market by an "imitate and improve" strategy.

How to innovate? Along product-differentiation lines marked by product-attribute dimensions. Conventional product differentiation strategies try to distinguish brands on the basis of "meaningful and highly valued" attributes. However, in many markets—particularly mature markets—attributes that *appear* to be valuable but upon examination are irrelevant can successfully work for product differentiation purposes. Carpenter and Nakamoto (1994) call this "meaningless differentiation"; if consumers are not aware of a differentiating attribute's true irrelevance, "they may incorrectly infer or *learn* that the unique attribute is associated with a satisfactory brand" and thus develop a preference for that attribute and the differentiated brand (for example, Perdue-brand chicken's yellow color). (I would prefer a less pejorative term than "meaningless differentiation," one which recognizes the importance of affect as well as cognition in consumers' preference formation.) Once formed, these associations can be difficult for competitors or social critics to eliminate from consideration (and they are almost impossible for a competitor to duplicate without appearing to be a pure imitation)—even if consumers learn over time that the differentiating attribute is truly irrelevant. In fact, this meaningless differentiation may continue to be used by the pioneer successfully even though consumers *acknowledge* the attribute's true (objective) irrelevance. The attribute may tap into deep affect, or simply have become a habit for consumers, both of which may be crucially important to the consumer at some level. Regardless, this becomes an extremely defendable barrier against later entrants getting into the market and successfully challenging the pioneer's position.

Later Entrant Approaches

The best approach for a later entrant, conclusively demonstrated by many of Schnaars's (1994) case studies, is to imitate and improve the pioneer's product. Pure imitation—blatant knockoffs—do not work well, nor does simply stating "We're just as good as the pioneer, only cheaper"—unless the later entrant can also expand the market substantially by lowering the price of the product (as in microwave ovens, which went through two waves of lowering prices—first by the Japanese, who drove out American manufacturers, then by the Koreans, who drove out the Japanese). Although many of Schnaars's examples of "imitate and improve" are from the recent past of high-tech products, other examples come readily to mind. And, of course, the later entrant has a decided cost advantage in much lower R&D expenditures, which probably negates some of the concern about entering early to jump on the so-called experience curve effects. (See Jellinek and Schoonhoven [1994] for an in-depth examination of these concerns in five firms and their impact on the semiconductor market in the United States.)

The later entrant usually need not be in a great hurry to enter the market, either; there is no need for a "fast second." A period of watchful waiting usually is not a hazard, for many products fall into a "long, long useless stage" (see Table 2.2). In fact, this stage was

TABLE 2.2. Products Stuck in a Long, Long Useless Stage

Product	Years Between First Appearance and Commercial Acceptance
35mm cameras	40
Ballpoint pens	8
Credit/charge cards	8
Diet soft drinks	10
Light beer	9
Mainframe computers	10
Microwave ovens	20
Nonalcoholic beer	6
Paperback books	5
Personal computers	6
Answering machines	15
VCRs	20
Video games	13
Warehouse clubs	7

Source: Schnaars (1994), p. 197.

identified as long ago as 1935 (Gilfillan, 1935, cited in Schnaars, 1994). This long lag between product introduction and product success (or adoption) is the stage where many pioneers fail and the later entrants that Schnaars has identified have taken over as market leader.

So—Now Where Are We?

Certainly not back at the very beginning. As marketers, we are typically handed a product situation and asked to help our client or company market it. Sometimes our client or company has an innovative product, but few of our clients or companies are truly market dominant. They need help in defending against later entry by bigger competitors. Continued improvement to that innovative product and a marketing approach which seeks to differentiate their product's attributes (however meaningless and irrelevant they may be objectively) is the best defense we have to offer. Sometimes our firms seek to counter an innovation by a competitor. In this case, the best strategy would probably be watchful waiting and time the entry as the market starts to expand.

Having decided to target a market or markets, we now face the task of actually doing the segmenting, the dividing up of the market into discrete groups. The ways for doing so and the techniques for the job are the subject of the next chapter.

PART II:
SEGMENTATION STRATEGIES

Chapter 3

Physical Attribute Segmentation

Segmentation–the dividing of a total market into its component parts by some scheme (various methods will be described here and in the next two chapters)–is not new. It has been around as a marketing tool for so long that a countervailing wisdom developed almost twenty years ago that, for some products and services, the provider should not segment, that segmentation was too expensive to be worth doing. As a general rule, however, marketers in the last generation have segmented their markets more often than not; Wilkie and Cohen (1977) trace almost twenty years of research up to that time. In fact, at times marketers have probably oversegmented their markets. Weinstein (1987:3) calls segmentation "the key to marketing success," a statement he continues in his revised edition (1994:2), where he also discusses the "segmentation imperative." We are now inundated with dozens of varieties of various products that, until recently, would probably not have existed or–if they did exist–would have been marketed under different brands. (There has been a literature developed in the last few years bitterly condemning what are called "brand extensions"–where a brand name is used on products that are different from the original: Coke begets Diet Coke begets Caffeine-Free Diet Coke begets Cherry Coke, etc. In the process, the original product can get lost and the "franchise" built up over the years can be diluted. In the case of Miller Lite it is often claimed that the success of this extension all but destroyed the original Miller High Life.)

When faced with the concept of segmentation for the first time, undergraduate students usually decide that the basis for segmentation is by differences: what makes Group A different from Group B. However, what is more important–certainly for a pragmatic marketing application—is similarities: what makes the members of Group A more like each other than like the members of Group B. This allows us, using one or more of several statistical techniques, to cluster the respondents into groups, and then target our appeals to the members of one or more particular groups. Although little work has been done on the theory of segmentation, Mills (1981) delved into individuation/deindividuation theory as a means to explore communicating with the "mass" in a particular segment.

Segmentation schemes can be divided into two large groupings: those based upon physical attributes (geographics, demographics, and the combination of the two, geodemographics) and those based upon behavioral attributes of the customers (lifestyle, life stage, psychographics, and usage).

Geographic segmentation schemes are probably the oldest segmentation method of all. At its root, it assumes that people have needs because of where they live that are different from those of people who live elsewhere. The old saw about selling refrigerators to the Eskimos is a recognition of geographical segmentation's underlying principle. Because we are seeking to group like with like, geographical segmentation has a lot to recommend; it is simple to understand, simple to perform and implement, and simple to manage. An example of geographic segmentation might be a chain of motels, with properties scattered from coast to coast, to the mountains, and in urban areas. Some of the properties might be in Florida, where their prime season of attractiveness would be between Thanksgiving and Easter; others might be in northern states, where the prime season might be summer. Given the geographic dispersal, with its attendant seasonal variations, the chain can no longer market all of its properties as identical, even if they are physically alike. The Florida properties would be advertised as winter attractions, with those aspects emphasized that work well in such marketing—warm weather, outdoor attractions, proximity to the ocean—all of which serve to whet the appetites of those of us whose winter experience is dominated by snow and cold. The Northern properties could emphasize the fact that many of the things that people like to do in summer can be done outside, without having to worry about whether the air conditioner is going to work—tennis, golf, biking, and similar activities which become almost impossible in the Sun

Belt because of daytime temperatures above ninety degrees. Simple geographic segmentation is often the best and least expensive method to deal with a market. The drawback to geographical segmentation is that it is not customer-driven; rather, it is driven by the reality of the offering.

Demographic segmentation is the second-oldest consumer segmentation scheme. This is the old Bureau of the Census approach: designation by race, creed, color, sex, national origin, age, ability, and income. Demographic segmentation operates on the theory that people who have similar physical characteristics operate similarly. While the "truth" of this statement is obvious to anyone who has observed movies or television shows about teenagers, one must handle this type of segmentation very carefully, on every variable.

While it may be true that women do something differently from men, or teenagers from those in their sixties, in reality it is *most* women or *many* teenagers, not all of them. Those teenagers who do something more like those in their sixties might not like to be reminded that they do not fit with their peers–and those who do fit with their peers may resent the stereotyping. Probably the most famous demographic group–the Baby Boomer generation, born between 1946 and 1964–certainly has this difficulty. The Baby Boomer generation is really at least two different groups, split by "leading edge" and "trailing edge," having to do with whether they were of an age to be drafted and sent to Vietnam–or perhaps some other criterion, depending upon the analyst.

A demographic variable of interest is birth order. (However, I suspect these variables can only be used as descriptive, because I know of no way to focus messages on the individuals.) Claxton (1995) investigates the research done on birth order and concludes that, while it probably will never be a sole segmentation variable, birth order may be an important variable. Particularly given the trend toward smaller families, there will be a larger percentage of first children and more only children; this may be more important for product and service planning than segmentation, per se.

The truth of the danger of stereotyping that lurks within demographic segmentation schemes is made clearer when one remembers the continuing uproar over malt liquor, a beer product largely targeted to black consumers. Critics of advertising have complained for years that black faces were not present in advertisements in anything resembling their percentage in the population. Pollay, Lee, and Carter-Whitney (1992) found that blacks were first underadvertised to and then overadvertised to (comparing advertisements for cigarettes in *Ebony* to those in *Life).* Further, they were not offered filter cigarettes until years after they were advertised to whites. When predominantly black actors have been used for malt liquor ads, critics have responded on two fronts. First, the product should not be targeted to a community which has a perceived problem with alcohol by using attractive images surrounding the consumption of what is essentially high-alcohol beer. Second, not all blacks drink and thus the advertisements foster negative stereotypes of black males. Kaufman (1995) also reminds us of this point as it applies to the physically disabled. Ferrell (1985) focuses our attention on the ethics of the advertisements written and produced to call the attention of our target market segment(s) to our offering.

A set of mostly demographic variables that has been around in social science research and the popular press for decades is "social class." It is conceptually complex, philosophically unsettling, and—at least in the United States—methodologically challenging. (After all, "Not Our Kind, Dear" may work in a stable, hierarchical society—for instance late Victorian or Edwardian England—but how can it work in the United States where we typically view "class" as income-related?) However, in descriptive terms at least, it continues to offer insight into consumption choices (Coleman, 1983). Page (1992) outlines theories about conspicuous consumption and its roots in individuals and societies, although her paper concentrates on the United States. She then starts the history of the subject with Thorstein Veblen's *The Theory of the Leisure Class* and proceeds to outline the rest of the twentieth century's high consumption periods, ending with the yuppification of the 1980s. The article culminates with a hopeful statement that "Veblen's depiction of ostentatious display solely for reasons of invidious distinction" is gone; instead, societies "tastefully consume to denote belongingness to a particular group" (p. 86). Mason (1992) proceeds to develop a conceptual model for status goods, exploring the search, evaluation, and selection processes by which status goods are purchased and consumed. The model is firmly grounded in the research on symbolic and social consumption of goods and services—to be expected when one deals with goods whose "value" exceeds their purchase price. Mason then discusses the propensity to consume for status, for the purposes of display and social gain, thus placing this consumption clearly in the social arena, moving the model from the strictly individual orientation of most models of consumer behavior. Although this model is a conceptual one, and thus highly theoretical, I believe that it is necessary to understand it in order to understand some of the processes by which consumers come to the purchase of many goods and services, and not just those normally thought of as "status." One needs to remember that the word "status" not only connotes "elite" but also "rank or position" in a hierarchy or society. Therefore, many items which proclaim one's position are purchased "socially" and not "individually." Or, perhaps, to signify one's social class.

A relatively recent development in demographic marketing is the so-called "mature" market—senior citizens, golden agers, or whatever. Moschis (1992, 1993) has categorized this group (those fifty-five and up) into four segments based on health and consumption patterns rather than on age. As the Baby Boomers age, the fifty-five and over segment will become even larger; a scheme to break it down on some basis will surely become more important. According to Davis and French (1989), the "mature" age group is now so large and complex that only psychographics can be used to segment it into the smaller segments necessary to market to the different submarkets.

The fact that the first Baby Boomers turned fifty in 1996 has led to some serious handwringing and consideration of the impact of the over-fifty market for the first time for many companies. Club Med, the quintessential "swinging singles" company of times past (far past in reality, but not necessarily in perception), found that it had misread the mature market even before the Baby Boomer generation which started Club Med's success got there, and its "Forever Young" program suffered as a result, until the firm had done its research. They discovered, for one thing, that the mature customers were bringing their grandchildren (possibly without their children; anyone who strolls through theme parks on a summer day will observe the phenomenon of grandparents and grandchildren without the intervening generation—and not a few of these units, either);

family reunions turned out to be an important market for Club Med (Miller, 1996).

The targeting of mature markets may pose a problem for marketers for the foreseeable future (Wolfe, 1992). Advertising agencies are typically populated by young people (particularly on their creative staffs) and they often have trouble seeing outside their upper-middle-class young adult selves. As Richard Lee, an agency veteran, put it "this business has always been self-centered, but we didn't notice because the attention was on the boomer generation" (Miller, 1996:6). As the Baby Boomers age and the agency population does not (the "Mr. Chips Factor"), this dichotomy has become noticeable and will become more so and more dangerous to marketers.

Further, the report of a recent survey of women's views of themselves and advertising reminds us of the power–albeit of a negative sort–of stereotypes (Beatty, 1995). Sexist stereotypes are disappearing, but the "vast majority of women" that Grey Advertising surveyed said that "advertising is more unrealistic today than it was even two years ago"–80 percent said that the home life portrayed in ads is unrealistic versus 70 percent two years ago. Marketers are blamed for still "seeing women as one-dimensional." Too often, marketers view women as women, rather than women as people. According to Beatty, women are the largest purchasers of educational software and hardware for children and represent the fastest-growing segment of business owners, thus potential purchasers of equipment normally marketed at men. It would seem, therefore, that sex is not a good segmentation variable, except for products which *specifically* are used by women, such as feminine hygiene products, or by men, such as prostate medications. Demographic segmentation, thus, has drawbacks.

Nevertheless, demographic segmentation has great potential for targeting audiences at relatively low cost or difficulty, and has the added bonus that it is aimed not at the producer or product, but at something about the customer. Probably the demographic variable that most lends itself to credible, useful segmentation and targeting is age. Although not all teenagers are alike, any more than all women are alike, certain products and services can be offered to age groups who have higher propensities to consume them than other groups. In fact, Longfellow and Celuch (1993) report on a segmentation scheme based upon the degree to which they are willing to be involved in the service being provided.

At opposite ends of the age spectrum, children and "senior citizens" are most often treated as specific entities by marketers. Why? Because they have behavioral characteristics in common with others in their own age cohort that allow for easy separation from other age cohorts. Young children, for example, have little money of their own to spend, but a great deal of influence on purchasers of goods and services intended for them. Toys, games, movies, and fast food are only a few of the examples which come immediately to mind. Coca-Cola has recently targeted children as part of their effort to reintroduce the "classic-shaped" bottle (Egol, 1996). As children get older, they get more money to spend on themselves and as the children become teenagers, they attract enormous attention from clothing manufacturers, CD producers, movie producers, and college admissions personnel, to name just a few. (See McNeal [1987] for a discussion of the ethical pitfalls in dealing with children as consumers.) A whole subculture has developed around the large tribe known as teenagers; it has created several media avenues for communicating with them—many with their own codes, cues, and taboos—some of which are psychically or emotionally painful for adults to view or use. Hassan and Katsanis (1994) report on global segmentation of teenagers; they found that teenagers are more alike worldwide then they are like another group.

At the other end of the age spectrum, "senior citizens"–variously defined as those over fifty-five, over sixty, over sixty-five, etc.–have become a recognized demographic market of their own. As a group, they have a lot of discretionary money (not necessarily "income") to spend on goods and services that appeal to them (including items for their grandchildren; see the segment mentioned above). Many, many businesses have already realized the easy segmentation and targetability of this group; the American Association of Retired Persons rents its list of members (age fifty-five and above). Of course, "senior citizens" are no more a single group than any other. There are different groups within this umbrella based on age, physical abilities, behavior, and so forth.

Nevertheless, senior citizens are frequently targeted. Senior citizens are often targeted negatively; many scams are aimed directly at older consumers on the grounds that they are less sophisticated and probably less mentally alert and will thus easily fall prey to dishonest marketing. They are also often targeted positively with discounts. Why senior citizens should be given a price reduction simply based on age has always baffled me. On the same trip to my in-laws mentioned in Chapter 1 of this book, I witnessed my father-in-law receiving a discount of anywhere from 10 percent to 20 percent on dinners (he ate more than I), museum admissions, and miniature golf. Some of these discounts are undoubtedly predicated on the premise that seniors represent incremental business. However, all too often, seniors will not go somewhere without such a discount; this promotion has become as prevalent and corrosive of profits and marketing good sense as cents-off coupons for packaged goods. It is unjustifiable on any economic analysis except the old adage, "my competitors do it and I'll go out of business if I don't match it." In terms of the use of demographics to segment the market for hotel rooms, the implications are easy to see. First, properties can be designed to appeal to families with children (or conversely, *not* to appeal to them by excluding) by including playgrounds, children's menus in the dining room (the aspect of the Holiday Inn which first caught my mother's eye), children staying free, and so on. Seniors can be given discounts. Perhaps both ends of the age spectrum can be excluded from the target market by not Including playgrounds and the other aspects of the hotel which appeal to families with children or seniors, or by scheduling attractions that are not family-friendly, as Las Vegas used to do. These actions should reduce the number of guests outside the target market.

Demographic variables that can be used for segmentation and targeting purposes include more than just age, of course. Height and/or weight can work. Tall men's clothing stores and tall women's clothing stores are not new; rarer are stores for short men, although stores for short and petite women are not really new. These segments are attractive for catalogue vendors. Race works for certain products as does religion. Handled properly, with a great deal of discretion and understanding, any demographic variable is useable. The problem may lie in reaching the desired segment without offending either it or any other segment who might see your message.

Both geographic segmentation and demographic segmentation are relatively easy and inexpensive; however, they both suffer from pitfalls. By combining the two into what is tongue twistingly called "geodemographics," marketers have reinforced their strengths and tried to minimize their weaknesses. Much of the current brief for geodemographic segmentation comes from a combination of two factors: the sense that too often marketers strive for "elegance" at the expense of simplicity and cost-effectiveness, plus the rapid and continuing decline in the price of desktop computers, particularly in regard to their increasing power.

In the mid-1970s I was the assistant credit manager at Medusa Cement Company, then a large purveyor of cement and mortar, with six plants, sales of over $120 million, and seven sales districts, each with at least six salesmen. One of the people in the marketing department at headquarters spent a large amount of her time redoing sales territory maps by hand.

Cement is of low value and is sold by weight. Since it is heavy, it cannot be shipped profitably very far from the plant. Each cement plant has a "natural monopoly" of territory surrounding it; the extent of that monopoly is impinged upon by neighboring plants. As prices—determined in those days by an arcane base price plus shipping—fluctuated slightly, the natural territories expanded and contracted around each plant. Each time this happened, Mary Anne had to completely redo the map for the sales district around that plant—by hand. When the price fluctuated again—which it was sure to do—she had to redraw the map again. The fact that I never saw one of these maps being used by anyone besides the head of market research seemed not to matter to anyone. Mary Anne had to redraw these maps time and time again.

Was there a better way to perform this task? Don't ask about Medusa's computer; the machine that was in use in those dim days of yore was not capable of performing some of the financial calculations of the trusty Texas Instruments "Business Analyst," which got me through my MBA finance classes. Therefore, the answer possibly is that at the time, if these maps were important, Mary Anne had to redraw them—by hand. Today, however, most desktop personal computers could do what Mary Anne did, faster, more accurately, and without complaining about having to do the job. Desktop computers have led to a rebirth of geodemographic segmentation, more frequently called market mapping (Baker and Baker, 1993).

All of this discussion leads to the question of who should use market mapping. Traditional—that is, noncomputer (or at least mainframe computer)—users of mapping have been retail and franchise operations seeking store locations, manufacturers looking for plant sites or warehouse locations, banks trying to site branches in profitable neighborhoods within a framework of regulatory requirements for branch location, and, of course, firms trying to draw sales territories on some scientific, rational (or at least equitable) basis. Now, all of these traditional users can benefit from the desktop revolution of ease of use and rapidity of turnaround of analyses; so can other, nontraditional, users.

Of what use are geodemographics? They are all based on the concept that "birds of a feather flock together"—that is, we are more similar to those who live around us than we are dissimilar, or—as Weiss (1994:9) states, "where we live affects our attitudes toward what we buy. . . ." I think that although this may be true, it reverses the direction of major causality; the statement should read "what we think influences where we live"—at least at the micro level.

Nevertheless, Weiss (1994) uses market mapping to highlight the 211 consumer markets in the United States, usually in terms of markets that purchase an item above and below the U.S. average. He then summarizes the markets. Of Cleveland, he states that "nothing about Cleveland truly stands out. With its average incomes, home values, and education levels, Ohio's largest city [not true when the book was published] stays near the mean on consuming everything from books and stocks to motorcycles and pets" (Weiss, 1994:119). Although this is probably true, the rest of the description is rather dated and elitist. But more damning, the "Cleveland" market includes Akron, Canton, Youngstown, Lorain, and most of the rest of Northeastern Ohio—hardly a homogeneous market, as all of these cities are centers of their own metropolitan markets. In short, these 211 "consumer markets" are geographically too large, averaging over 1 million people in each—and the Cleveland market as defined contains over 3 million.

Jonathan Robbin created PRIZM (Potential Rating Index for Zip Markets) on the basis that where people lived and who they lived among told a lot about them. PRIZM is a system—originally of forty clusters, now sixty-two—where each zip code can be represented as belonging to a cluster which has a personality of its own (see Table 3.1 for a list). This boils down to "you are where you live," but not in the sense that Clevelanders are all alike. In fact, a zip code in Cleveland may have more in common with a zip code in San Diego than with other zips in Cleveland (Weiss, 1988).

As attractive as this concept is—for one thing, it is easy to deal with as the Postal Service provides the zip code for every address in the United States—it has some problems. First is the fact that, as I said earlier, I believe that it reverses cause and effect. Second, areas zip codes cover are extremely large. I live in 44120; half of this zip is in the city of Cleveland, the remainder is in Shaker Heights, a Cleveland suburb. It comprises tens of thousands of people of all races, religions, and economic standing, ranging from housing projects in Cleveland to some of the wealthiest people in Ohio—and a lot in between. The median house price in the Cleveland market is around $80,000 as I write this; the median house in the Shaker Heights part of 44120 has to exceed $160,000, the median price in the Cleveland portion would be considerably less than $80,000. I have seen analyses of the zip code done by PRIZM while testing the potential use of the system for a client; I know enough about the area encompassed by the zip code to be less than impressed with the results PRIZM produced. It is possible now to reduce the zip code to "carrier route" (zip+4—the nine-digit zip code), reducing the size and population of the cluster; however, this simultaneously makes administration of the system more difficult. PRIZM bears a parentage in direct marketing and mail targeting; although it is attractive enough at first glance, until a system can come down to a manageable number of households, it is too cumbersome to use for much beyond direct mail.

How would geodemographic segmentation be used? Targeting direct-marketing solicitations is an obvious case. If a motel had decided that it wanted only upscale guests, it would rent a mailing list (or a list of magazine subscribers to insert an advertisement aimed only to them) that had been drawn only from the clusters such as Blue Blood Estates, Money and Brains, Furs and Station Wagons, or Urban Gold Coast to ensure that a large percentage of the house-

TABLE 3.1. America's 40 Neighborhood Types (PRIZM)

Blue Blood Estates	America's wealthiest suburbs
Money and Brains	Posh, urban enclaves
Furs and Station Wagons	New money in suburbs
Urban Gold Coast	Upscale, urban high-rises
Pools and Patios	Older, upper-middle-class suburbs
Two More Rungs	Comfortable, multi-ethnic suburbs
Young Influentials	Yuppie fringes
Young Suburbia	Child-rearing, outlying suburbs
God's Country	Upscale, frontier boomtowns
Blue-Chip Blues	Wealthiest blue-collar suburbs
Bohemian Mix	Inner-city, bohemian enclaves
Levittown, USA	Aging, post-World War II tract subdivisions
Gray Power	Upper-middle-class, retirement communities
Black Enterprise	Predominantly black, middle-class neighborhoods
New Beginnings	Fringe city, mixed-housing areas
Blue-Collar Nursery	Middle-class, child-rearing towns
New Homesteaders	New Immigrant neighborhoods
New Melting Pot	America's college towns
Towns and Gowns	Older, blue-collar, industrial suburbs

44

Rank and File	Midscale, midsize towns
Middle America	Working class, rowhouse districts
Old Yankee Rows	Small towns based on light industry and farming
Coalburg and Coaltown	Crossroads villages
Shotguns and Pickups	Cottage communities
Golden Ponds	Small towns, surrounded by ranches and large farms
Agri-business	Predominantly black, working-class neighborhoods
Emergent Minorities	Downscale, urban-singles districts
Single City Blues	Struggling steeltowns and mining villages
Mines and Mills	Remote, downscale farm towns
Back-Country Folks	Lower-middle-class milltowns and industrial suburbs
Norma Rae-Ville	Inner-city districts of small cities
Smalltown Downtown	The nation's most sparsely populated rural areas
Grain Belt	Lower-working-class districts, in older, industrial cities
Heavy Industry	Southern farming and light industry areas
Share Croppers	Aging, predominantly black neighborhoods
Downtown Dixie Style	America's Hispanic barrios
Hispanic Mix	Predominantly black, southern farm communities
Tobacco Roads	The nation's poorest rural areas
Hard Scrabble	America's inner-city ghettos

Source: Weiss (1988), pp. 4-5.

45

holds who received the solicitation were upscale. Of course, this would miss many upscale families who did not live in the "right" zip code and catch many nonupscale families who did, for one reason or another. The same technique can be utilized for cable television, as cable operators hold franchises from specific munici-palities and potential advertisers can buy advertising slots for spe-cific municipalities. Although this may not be "clean"–Shaker Heights, for instance, contains parts of three zip codes which may not all be in the same PRIZM group–it is more targeted than just broadcasting.

In a generic sense, the geodemographic databases are becoming more sophisticated over time. They can provide a tremendous amount of detail necessary for site selection for retail and restaurant loca-tions, if nothing else. They are, however, not a panacea; they repre-sent only the first pass through a wealth of information (O'Malley, Patterson, and Evans, 1995). I have a client who produces several local newspapers, distributed community-wide or by zip code. Fur-ther, he has produced a "lifestyle" newspaper aimed at several zip codes away from the core newspaper in the area. We have tried using geodemographics to get new subscribers, but have found the technique unwieldy to date–nevertheless, we keep looking.

Chapter 4

Behavioral Attribute Segmentation

Lifestyle segmentation, the first of the segmentation methods based on behavioral traits, is predicated upon the presumption that people who do similar things will buy similar things. Kassarjian (1971) reviewed the state of the literature a generation ago to see what the state of the field of personality and consumer behavior was; he concluded that it was equivocal.

Rather than the "race, creed, and color" of demographic segmentation schemes, lifestyle segmentation is based upon "activities, interests, and opinions," some of which—obviously—reflect one's personality. This is a rather attractive scheme for segmenting many markets: It is rather obvious, not difficult to do, and communicating to the target segment(s) is not difficult today, given the proliferation of special interest media, particularly magazines. It seems as if there is at least one magazine for any particular interest group, no matter how obscure or bizarre. Lastovicka (1982) reviewed the literature, however, and discovered that there was little published evidence to suggest that lifestyle trait researchers had rigorously tested its validity; in a test in the article, his results only partially supported its validity. Bryant (1986), however, reviewed several practitioner-driven surveys which discovered lifestyle characteristics and traits that aided in delivering a more targeted message. Much of the difference in findings between Lastovicka (1982) and Bryant (1986) has to be the difference between academic and practitioner outlook. Bryant claims that lifestyle segmentation research can be used to gain insights on consumer motivation, for turning on creative ideas, and as an enrichment to demographic or geodemographic segmentation schemes. He does not claim *validity* for the concept, only that it seems to work.

There are few doubters about lifestyle and its impact on marketing. Barnett (1986:40) is one; however, he is an anthropologist and not a marketer. He claims that most people do not "actually live a life style, they desperately try to live up to a life style." Lifestyles are "more models of how we are supposed to think and act than descriptions of the complexities, contradictions, ambiguities, quirks and eccentricities of our everyday lives." Although to a certain extent he is correct, what he is describing is a model, and models are always simplifications. The question here is less "Is the Model an Accurate Representation of Life?" than "Does the Model Look Like How I Live?" Perception counts here much more than "objective" reality. Over twenty years ago Plummer (1974:36-37) listed several benefits of lifestyle segmentation:

1. Redefinition of key target(s)
2. Provide a new view of market
3. Product positioning
4. Better focus marketing communications
5. Develop sounder overall marketing and media strategies
6. Suggest new product opportunities
7. Explains the "why" of a product situation

Although much of this list could be as true of any type of segmentation scheme, Plummer's contention is that it is exceptionally true for lifestyle segmentation. And, I would add, true even if Barnett's analysis that there is no such thing as a lifestyle is correct.

Although it should be relatively apparent how to segment by some lifestyle characteristics, I would like to discuss two rather divergent characteristics to show how powerful a tool lifestyle segmentation can be, if the right characteristics are chosen and the wants and needs of those whose lifestyle they fit can be found, communicated with, and convinced that your firm is taking care of those wants and needs.

The first of these characteristics is based upon time and time pressure. Our Western fascination with time and our peculiarly American desire to "save" time does not come without a price, particularly as electronic means of communicating across great distances in real time proliferate—we can always be on call and be expected to respond to that call (Valeriano, 1991; Hirsch, 1991); this is a reality that physicians have had to deal with for years, but the rest of us are just beginning to get swept up in the pager/voice mail maelstrom. It has become a truism in the 1990s that we are all time stressed and desperate to slow down; although this is a truism for both men and women, it is allegedly even more true for women (Michman, 1991:149, heads a section "Poverty of Time and the New Role of Women"). This is popularly referred to as the result of the "Supermom Syndrome" and currently a backlash is being reported to that syndrome (Lublin, 1995). In a study for Hilton Hotels, one-half of the 1,000 people questioned said they would take one day a week off without pay to get more time (Hymowitz, 1991). This time pressure has become a problem around the great American consumption ritual of Christmas (Miyazaki, 1993). American's attitudes toward available time are displayed in Table 4.1.

But truisms are not always true. There have been many recent reports about the amount of free time or leisure time available today in comparison with the past. In the space of less than eighteen months, *American Demographics* ran three major articles on the subject. Robinson (1989) used time-use diaries from the Survey Research Center at the University of Maryland to compare the number of hours of free per week in 1965, 1975, and 1985; he found that there was basically no change for men and that women had increased their free time from thirty-four to thirty-nine hours per week over that span. However, there are great differences in the amount of free time between marrieds and unmarrieds of both sexes; further the group thirty-six to fifty years of age has dramatically less time than those either eighteen to thirty-five or fifty-one to sixty-four (partly, at least, the result of higher parental responsibilities in the middle group).

Robinson (1990) reported on perception data from subjective questions about time included in the diary studies cited in the above paragraph. Here the results are quite different; basically the question was: "Do you ever feel rushed to do things?" Among those eighteen to sixty-four, 32 percent reported in 1985 that they always feel rushed, compared to 28 percent in 1975 and 25 percent in 1965. When Robinson compared the data from the diaries to the subjective question he found (no surprise) that those feeling rushed work more

TABLE 4.1. Goals and Attitudes Toward Time

Goals for the 1990s

77%	Spend time with family and friends
74%	Improve self intellectually, emotionally, or physically
72%	Save money
66%	Have free time to spend any way you please
61%	Make money
59%	Pursue personal experiences such as traveling and hobbies

Feeling Squeezed for Time

38%	Report cutting back on sleep to make more time
33%	Say they are unlikely to be able to make time for their ideal weekend
31%	Worry they don't spend enough time with family and friends
20%	Report calling in sick to work at least once during the past twelve months to simply get time off

Trading Pay for Free Time

| 70% | Of those earning $30,000 a year or more would give up a day's pay each week for an extra day off |
| 48% | Of those earning $20,000 a year or less would do the same |

Women Feel More Pressure

36%	Of the women responding often feel at the end of the day that they haven't accomplished what they set out to do
28%	Of the men responding say they often feel the same way
35%	Of the women say they are constantly under stress— trying to accomplish more than they can handle
23%	Of the men responding say they feel the same stress

Source: Hymowitz (1991).

hours and spend more time caring for children than those who do not feel so rushed but spend no more time on housework or grocery shopping. (For a discussion of time consumed driving children from place to place, see O'Boyle, 1991.) They do spend more time on taking care of themselves, being involved in organizational activities and sports. The time-pressured seem to be classic type A personalities, cramming as much activity into their days as possible (Robinson, 1990:33).

Cutler (1990) reports that one reason people feel more time-pressed is that passive forms of leisure such as television are taking more hours out of their schedule (fifteen per week in 1985 compared to 10.5 in 1965). We have more leisure time, but thanks to TV's ability to fill the time and make it seem as though we are doing something, many do not appreciate or notice the difference (Cutler, 1990:36-37). For every hour of leisure time gained between 1965 and 1985, people spent another hour in front of the TV set (Newhouse News Service, 1991:3-A). This raises the question of what constitutes leisure time. Is the time pressure that is reported a result of a lack of "free" time *versus* a lack of "time off from work"? What would the difference between the two mean? Time off from work–particularly at night during the week–seems in the 1990s to mean time in front of the television. It is during the weekend that other activities take place. Is the source of some of the time pressure a result of frenetic weekends involving out-of-house activities?

> Even the economists have entered the fray. The presumption of declining leisure is in fact a fallacy. Previous studies purporting to have uncovered such a fact have not adequately disentangled time spent in home production activities such as meal preparation, laundry, home maintenance, or child care from time spent enjoying leisure activities. . . . Although the average worker is spending more time working for pay than in the past, this change has not come at the expense of leisure. It represents, instead, a shift from time spent in home production to time spent in market activities. (Roberts and Rupert, 1995:1)

Gene Epstein, in his column on the Roberts and Rupert report, headlined this as "Myth: Americans Are Working More; Fact: More Women Are Working" (Epstein, 1995:32). Despite the response that the Roberts and Rupert thesis has aroused anywhere it has been printed, what they are truly talking about is an analysis at the macro level; they are not talking about any individual's 168 hours during the week. I know one of the authors; his personal calendar has been altered dramatically in the past few years as he has changed careers from professor to economist at the Cleveland Federal Reserve Bank. He also has a four-year-old-daughter. The Roberts and Rupert analysis goes directly to the trading of home work for paid work by women (and, to some extent men) as their increasing affluence leads them to *buy* what an earlier generation *did*. Would an earlier generation have labelled cooking as a leisure activity? Would an earlier generation have labelled cutting the grass a leisure activity? Has our definition of leisure changed? Anderson et al. (1989) and Gronmo (1989) further show some of the changes that have occurred in the past decade, making one question whether any previous thesis on the subject is valid any longer.

It has been possible to discuss many items in advertising and other marketing settings as "time-saving" appliances. Gross and Sheth (1989:77) posited two research hypotheses about advertising appeals and time:

> H1: United States magazine advertising has made reference to time-oriented concerns and product benefits with increasing frequency during succeeding decades since the late 1800s (when the United States was largely an agrarian economy [a point which many economic historians would certainly dispute; we probably became an industrial economy long before 1890, which is what they seem to mean by late 1800s–what Gross and Sheth probably mean is we were not an urban society]).

> H2: Time-oriented appeals have been used as primary appeals with increasing frequency during succeeding decades since the late 1800s in contrast to their use as secondary or tertiary appeals.

Gross and Sheth performed content analysis on a sample of advertisements appearing in the *Ladies' Home Journal* over the past century and found that both hypotheses were confirmed–with the usual academic caveats. They contrasted this finding, a clear case where values communicated in advertising have changed over time, with Pollay's (1984) observation that values so communicated have changed only minimally over time. Leonard Berry talked about firms profiting by helping time-poor consumers to increase their stock of discretionary time as far back as 1979 (Berry, 1979). Anderson et al. (1989) developed a women's timestyle typology with eleven categories.

So, what to do? It is obvious that, despite academic and economists' critiques to the contrary, people feel time- stressed or time-pressured. As Leonard Berry states in a sidebar to Robinson's (1990) article mentioned earlier:

> Time diaries may be the most accurate way to measure how people actually spend their time, but it is perception that shapes behavior. People who believe they are pressed for time will act accordingly. The perception that time is scarce is resulting in "time-buying" behavior. . . . By trading dollars for time-saving goods and services and by shopping in time-efficient stores, consumers are doing just that. . . . The impact of perceived time scarcity extends to all types of retailers. In the 1990s, a store that wastes people's time will be committing competitive suicide. (Berry, 1990:32)

But products or services that waste people's time will be committing competitive suicide as well. "Convenient" has come to mean "quick." Not so long ago, frozen meals came in aluminum trays that could go directly from the freezer into the (conventional) oven; today they have to come in plastic microwavable containers so that no one has to be inconvenienced by transferring the food to another container and then having to wash that container. Microwavable foods are necessary because (following the Roberts and Rupert [1995] analysis above) we have decided to buy more of our food preparation for cash instead of spending the time to do it. Of course, when time is of the essence, even microwaving the family's dinner will take too long; in these circumstances, bringing precooked food home or going to a restaurant are the best ways to "save time," trends that are currently shaking up several industries as they fight for "share of stomach" (Saporito, 1995). Darian and Cohen (1995) report on a study that showed those who are the most "time-poor" do not use more "convenience foods" than those who are somewhat time-poor, but they do purchase more meals from restaurants. Their conclusions are that segmenting on an attribute such as "convenience" may be less profitable than segmenting along perceived time-pressure dimensions. Their findings are partially confirmed by a study conducted by NPD Group: households with women who work full time with children eat at a restaurant 10 percent more often than such households where the woman is not employed; however, disposable income does enter the equation as well, since households without children where the woman is employed eat at restaurants 30 percent more often than such households where the woman is not employed ("Mom's Munching Habits," 1995), although Saporito (1995) clearly indicates that the differences between fast-food restaurants, "casual-dining" restaurants, and grocery stores is blurring. As Rigdon (1991) points out, there may need to be a geographic element in the segmentation; there seem to be differences–at least between the East Coast and West Coast–in how time is used and, ultimately, perceived. And what about the "time-shifting" indulged in by those too busy to watch television shows at the time they are broadcast? The shows are taped on their VCRs in order to watch them at a time more suited to their schedules.

Time-shifting is one of the senses that several authors use in their discussions of "nontraditional" senses of time. (See, for example, Lane and Kaufman [n.d.,a,b]; Kaufman and Lane [n.d.,a,b]; Bluedorn, Kaufman, and Lane [1992]; Page, Wood, Kaufman, and Lane [1990].) They discuss a meeting between two businessmen as having two different intensities; not a different intensity for each person in some egocentric sense, but a physical intensity and a mental intensity which have different temporal dimensions. The physical intensity comes from the two businessmen being in the same room at the same time, trying to fit many tasks into a block of time when they are together; Lane and Kaufman then suggest that their level of mental intensity will increase after they separate and each attempts to define the meaning of the meeting and deal with post-meeting tasks apart from each other–which would lead to a lessening of their physical intensity. Some of the Kaufman and Lane analysis is supported by a semiotic analysis of time (Zerubavel, 1987). In this analysis, time becomes a "quasi-linguistic system of signification." This semiotic analysis explores how people use various dimensions of temporality such as duration, speed, frequency, and timing as semiotic codes through which they convey messages about priority, importance, commitment, respect and intimacy without having to verbalize these dimensions.

Great social science commentary, but what does any of this mean for segmentation? Continuing the "how do you chose a hotel" paradigm for this book, what does time do for a hotel attempting to segment its market? There are two diametrically opposed ways to segment the market(s) based on time. First, the business-oriented hotel operator can emphasize speed and ease of check-in and check-out, convenient location, ease and speed of access to the property, door-knob room service breakfast at any time selected, etc., all of which are rather obvious ways to remove the service delays that most business travelers find abhorrent. Other services such as in-room fax machines, computer facilities, and so forth are possible, but fraught with the danger that Valeriano (1991) and Hirsch (1991) pointed out and was mentioned earlier; executives may resent having these appliances of interruption as a reminder of being on a leash in the room. The hotel industry is responding to demand (not by their customers, but by those paying their customers' bills) and creating properties with rooms that "only a boss could love"—no lobbies, no fancy restaurants, but including business centers, in-room fax machines and personal computers (Bigness and Dahl, 1996).

Properties which are not aimed at business travelers, or at business travelers on vacation, can offer the same time-saving amenities (no one *likes* to stand in a check-out line), but not emphasize them. What the time-pressured customer may want when she or he is at leisure is different: perhaps an on-site spa, relaxing poolside food service, a slower tempo, no in-room fax or computer service, etc. How does one property attract both segments? This, of course, is always the difficult part of any segmentation strategy—the willingness to forgo business by excluding part of the market. However, rooms in different wings or on different floors could be designated "Executive" and "Club" with different layouts and different physical amenities.

The second lifestyle I would like to discuss as a potential segmenting variable is the so-called "Voluntary Simplicity" lifestyle. In this lifestyle one lives with a conscious appreciation of the condition of the rest of the world, giving up complexity; a practitioner of voluntary simplicity makes consumption choices based upon the view of the world as a holistic, ecological entity, that all things are connected. It is a statement that too much is too much, that as Americans we overconsume and that individuals can make a difference to the rest of the world by consuming less. It has nothing to do with poverty; it is *voluntary* restraint by those who could afford to do otherwise (Elgin, 1983; Steinhart, 1985). Leonard-Barton (1981) developed a six-factor voluntary simplicity scale and found that people who score high on the scale tend to be younger and more educated, but that there is no relationship with income or race. In other words, it is to all intents and purposes the opposite of the Yuppie lifestyle, so caricatured during the 1980s (Burnett and Bush, 1986). However, it is not monolithic; there are different types of people who practice voluntary simplicity and they do so for different reasons (Ensley, 1983). It is a lifestyle that may be developing more adherents throughout the 1990s (Martellaro, 1996).

As anticonsumption as Voluntary Simplicity appears, practitioners do not completely eschew consumption—only unnecessary or extravagant consumption. In fact, Beckett, McNutt, and Bahn (1994) call this "symbiotic" rather than "voluntary simplicity," which changes the tenor and removes the possibility of misunderstanding by those who market to this segment. These people will still travel, read, listen to music, etc. How to reach these people? They will be a relatively easy market to target, although any firm that wishes to have them as a target market should be ready to be rigorous in its standards of behavior; messages that are less than coherently simple will turn this segment off. How to get them to use a hotel property? Cutting the frills is obvious. This group will like windows that open so that heat and air conditioning can be turned off when not warranted, as well as unheated swimming pools, bicycles and other active recreation equipment for the guests to use, and vegetarian choices in the restaurant. The list is endless, but the message that the property managers need to convey is that they know and understand the lifestyle and, whether they personally approve or not, they do not find it a matter of amusement that their guests show up wearing backpacks riding bicycles rather than in a Mercedes carrying Louis Vuiton luggage.

There are other lifestyle variations which may prove to be attractive markets to target—or, conversely, to target to miss. The two above are offered solely as examples of the types of traits to look for when targeting. The overarching concerns are, as always: whether or not the target is big enough to be worth pursuing, whether or not we can organize our marketing and delivery efforts to garner the target's business and ensure that we do not offend their sensibilities, and whether or not the target can be reached readily with a good communications program. Whatever lifestyle variations you observe that seem to be segmentable and fit under these overarching concerns should be valid segmentation variables.

There is a bridge between Lifestyle Segmentation and the next strategy–Life Stage Segmentation–and that is the role of the family, both as a segmentation variable and as a target market. Much has been written in the past several years about the family and the changes it has undergone in the past generation as well as changes it will undoubtedly face in the future. Little of the ink spilled, however, is directly useable for the present purpose, for little of it addresses changes in the family as a buying unit.

Directing attention to the family as a buying unit is an obvious action to take and has clear appeal for many industries. Housing is directed primarily at families (although there is the beginning of a trend to provide owner-occupied housing for singles [Crump, 1995]). Life insurance is directed to people to provide for their families after they are gone. And so on. However, we are constantly reminded that these are the 1990s and the family has changed. The "traditional" family–which truly turns out to have been typical only of the families in which the Baby Boomers were raised–of father at work, mother at home, two-point-something children all living in a house by themselves–is no longer the dominant means of organizing a family, and marketers need to recognize this fact because it has tremendous implications for how goods and services will be delivered, bought, packaged, and consumed in the future.

The necessity for considering the family as family for marketers is to confront it as the decision-making unit. If the head of household is truly the target for a product, do not focus on the family; this may be the case for life insurance. The head of household is simply taking care of his or her obligations to dependents, not dealing with a family issue. Items such as houses, furniture, cars, college education, etc. are Much more apt to involve the family as decision-making units. Further, one must be careful to separate the buyer from the user of a product or service. One of the old war horses of teaching marketing was the fact that a very large percentage of take-away beer was bought by women; teachers could always get a knowing laugh from undergraduate marketing classes over the image of all those housewives guzzling beer. Of course, they were typically buying the beer at grocery stores for their husbands to drink.

A family-marketing approach extends the range of possible purchaser/consumer relationships in three dimensions: there can be more than one decision maker, more than one consumer, and these may be different people (Boutilier, 1993). Boutilier then describes what he calls the "drama" of family marketing, where people take roles as the Initiator of a purchase (who may not actually use or buy the product), the Influencer of a purchase, and the Purchaser (who may have nothing else to do with the product, like the beer-buying housewife of old).

Viewing the family purchasing process as a drama has tremendous descriptive power (see Grove and Fisk [1989, 1992] to see how the power of drama has been used similarly to focus on services marketing). If nothing else, addressing the family purchasing process as a drama adds the dimension of time to it. Family decision making typically takes more time than individual decision making, for there are more people whose needs and wants must be considered. In this aspect, family purchasing looks like organizational buying behavior (discussed in Chapter 5); the roles that Boutilier has assigned are directly from an organizational buyer-behavior model.

One difficulty here is dealing with the family as a family. It is obvious that there are purchasing decisions that are made as a family; some that come immediately to mind are for cars, houses, and vacations. The problem is that we know little about how the family as a family reaches decisions, who plays what role when. We know something about husband/wife dyads in the purchase process (Lavin, 1993), about the role that children often play, but there has been very little research on the family. Another difficulty is in communicating with the family as a family. If we segment along family lines, we need to be able to communicate to those segments as segments, and it is extremely unlikely that any medium will permit us to do so.

The obvious role of the family in the process makes it important to find out. My children often play roles of Influencer in the decision-making process–hissing Holiday Inns every time we pass one, for instance. Does the Initiator also become an Influencer? Purchaser? What if the Purchaser is not part of the family–as my father-in-law was when he made the reservations for us to stay in Daytona Beach? The difficulty in using the family as a segmentation variable is that communications plans have difficulty dealing with families rather than individual members; further, how do families exist in the diverse 1990s?

Are we just using the word "family" to substitute for "household"? This can be a problem. Fisher (1989) explicitly used lifestyle traits to fashion a "household production model" of the type that Roberts and Rupert (1995) used to discuss trading money for time; a more old-fashioned researcher might have labelled the model "family production model." What constitutes a family? Prior to my marriage, I lived with another single male in a two-bedroom apartment. We bought many things together, including groceries but not household durables (the danger in thus using household data and some procedures to deal with these aberrations is treated in Bayus and Mehta, 1994); were we a family? We were a household, certainly. But a family? It did not feel like one. The number of households grew 13 percent between 1980 and 1988–vastly exceeding the population growth of that period (Waldrop, 1989). Were they families or households?

Life-stage segmentation, also called the "family life cycle," is the recognition that a family's needs and expenditures change over time as people leave their parents' home, marry, have children, and grow up to repeat the cycle. In a sense, life-stage segmentation represents family demographics, particularly ages and income levels. The focus on longitudinal changes in purchases is valuable for predicting macro demand for specific product categories, such as houses, refrigerators, nursery sets, etc., although it can also be useful for dealing with demand for specific brands–or lack of demand. The advertising campaign "This is not your father's Oldsmobile" typifies the longitudinal, generational approach, as does Friedlander's (1975) categorization of lifestyles into "formalistic" (heavy reliance on higher authority for direction), "sociocentric" (looking to close intimate relationships for guidance and direction), and "personalistic" (looking inside for guidance and direction) based upon a sample of 1,154 individuals.

Life-stage analysis has commonly included the following eight categories (see Figure 4.1 for a graphic representation):

FIGURE 4.1. Family Life Cycles

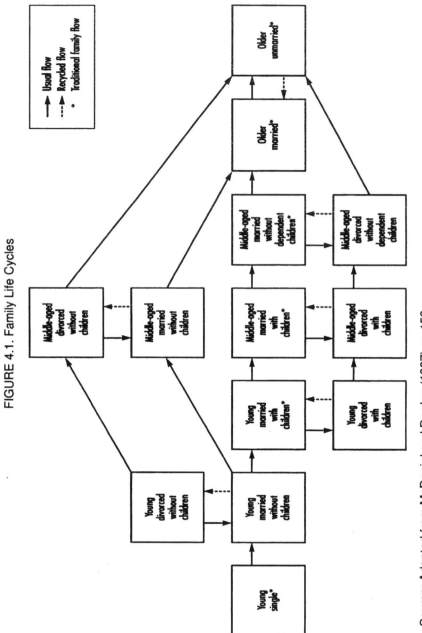

Legend:
→ Usual flow
⇢ Recycled flow
* Traditional family flow

Boxes: Young single* → Young married without children → Young married with children* → Middle-aged married with children* → Middle-aged married without dependent children* → Older married* → Older unmarried*

Young divorced without children; Young divorced with children; Middle-aged divorced without children; Middle-aged divorced with children; Middle-aged divorced without dependent children

Source: Adapted from McDaniel and Darden (1987), p. 152.

1. Young Single Stage–young is relative, but the title is now usually used to mean those who have never been married. This group has lower income than some of the others, but also has smaller financial responsibilities. This is the group frequently targeted for entertainment–ski vacation packages and similar products and services.

2. Newly Married Stage–still young (and childless). This is a relatively small group with substantial buying activity. This is the stage where houses and furnishings, white goods (stoves, refrigerators, etc.), dishes, and other consumer durables are bought in a relatively short time span.

3. Full Nest I Stage–children have appeared with the youngest not yet in school. Financial squeezing now truly appears; discretionary spending may be at its lowest point, particularly if one parent has not yet returned to the workforce or is employed part-time.

4. Full Nest II Stage–youngest child is now in school. Both parents are probably working (if this is intended), so the squeeze is reduced. Discretionary spending is still low, but purchases of children's goods and services are high.

5. Full Nest III Stage–the children are now teenagers. Expenditure patterns now represent the replacement of durables bought during the Newly Married Stage which have worn out or have become otherwise undesirable, as well as additional durables. Further, vacations and travel become more prevalent.

6. Empty Nest I Stage–the children have left home and entered their own Young Single Stage. The financial squeeze on the parents is over, leaving them free to travel, pursue hobbies, and substantially improve the house.

7. Empty Nest II Stage–the couple has retired and income has consequently declined. However, given the drastic reduction in necessary expenditures, discretionary expenditures may well be substantially increased. They may move to a smaller house or apartment, reducing the need to replace durables one more time; the second car may be foregone. However, spending on grandchildren may be quite high.

8. Solitary Survivor Stage–one partner is now widowed. Incomes again are low, as is financial responsibility, but medical expenses may absorb all of the previously discretionary income.

The explanatory power of the family life cycle concept is clear; it defines the trajectory of a family over time in terms of financial responsibilities and purchases as the makeup of the family changes. One may quibble that three "Full Nest Stages" are not necessary or that not everyone goes through every stage; however, a more damning weakness is obvious—this cycle describes the "traditional" family of *Leave It to Beaver* or Ozzie and Harriet Nelson. This is not the trajectory of the family of the 1990s.

The family of the 1990s is nothing if not diverse. College graduate children move back home, disrupting what would have been an Empty Nest. Composite families might have been Full Nest III, but after remarriage by the partners, now technically become Full Nest I because one of the (step)children is still not in school. Children go off to college and return to live at home after graduation or after a divorce (Johnson and Roberts, 1992). Divorce creates two families—one of which has no full-time children and only one adult, the other having the full-time children. And so on and so forth. These changes in family composition need to be recognized in any segmentation scheme which purports to deal with family life cycles.

Despite the great descriptive power of the concept of the family life cycle, communication with people in the various stages is difficult, since the stage may not coincide well with any demographic variable. Not only are many in the "Young Single Stage" older than Empty Nesters of any stage—and thus subject to being offended by the medium used to communicate with others in that stage—many in the "Solitary Survivor" stage are younger than Empty Nest II, with the same possibility. Or, as Tinney (1989) points out tongue-in-cheek, "Life Begins When the Kids Leave Home and the Dog Dies—But That's Where the Family Life Cycle Ends." She reminds us that not everyone over the median age is the same. Further, our children continue to influence our spending even after they are not part of the household—but remain part of the family. But we do keep trying (Lofland and Razzouk, 1992; Schaninger and Danko, 1993). Roberts, Voli, and Johnson (1992) redefine the concept a bit in a valiant and possibly fruitful attempt to separate "families" from "households." They do this by including the ages of the individuals in the household, the number of people present, the kinship situation(s) and psychic involvement(s) of the members, and the financial resource variables and the allocation involvement(s).

Further, other variables may be as predictive and descriptive. Goodwin and Lockshin (1992) suggest that marketers need to learn to adapt to consumers who present themselves alone to shop, to eat in restaurants, to travel. Marketers have failed to do so very well to date. Are solo consumers lonely or are they simply alone? As the family changes composition, with several stages where someone may be a solo "family"–from a young unmarried to a recently divorced or widowed individual, to an elderly survivor–these solo consumers will have different wants and needs that marketers need to be aware of. However, communicating with solo consumers will always be difficult; this is an instance where a segmentation scheme needs to be descriptive rather than predictive.

Without the ability to communicate easily with people in a segment while excluding those who do not belong in that segment, a scheme loses applicability. Thus, an interesting exploration into segmentation based upon the Luscher Color Test–an attempt to link the test back to psychographic profiles (Rogers, Slama, and Williams, 1983)–fails in the practicality test because, no matter how effective the results, they cannot be used well to communicate with the segments, which is part of the goal of any segmentation scheme.

Psychographic segmentation has been around for more than a generation (Demby, 1989); it uses lifestyle, social class, values, attitudes, and other psychological attributes–often overlaid atop some basic demographic data–to create multiple segments. At its heart, psychographics says that what people think and believe, the values they hold, and how they live and spend their money allows researchers a window into their behavior. It is a quantitative technique used to convey what is basically fuzzy, "touchy-feely" data about consumers (Demby, 1974). Probably the most famous "psychographic" segmentation scheme was VALS (Values and Life Style, produced by SRI, formerly Stanford Research International), which was not truly a psychographic segmentation scheme at all (more about VALS later).

The biggest factors that psychographics add to demographics are attitudes and values. According to the grandfather of values research in the social sciences, an attitude is an "enduring organization of several beliefs focused on a specific object . . . predisposing one to respond in some preferential manner." Values, on the other hand, "transcend specific objects and situations: values have to do with *modes of conduct* and *end-states of existence*" (Rokeach, 1968-1969:550). Put another way, a value is a type of belief centrally located within one's total belief system, about how one ought or ought not to behave (Rokeach, 1968). The "ultimate function of human values is to provide us with a set of standards to guide us in all our efforts to satisfy our needs. . . " (Rokeach, 1979:48). Obviously, values and attitudes are important to us, even though we do not yet know how they work (Spates, 1983).

Values and attitudes can and do change; values may be "enduring," but they are not immutable. They can change through creation, relatively sudden destruction, attenuation, extension, elaboration, specification, limitation, explication, consistency, and intensity (Williams, 1967; 1979); or acquisition, redistribution, rescaling of commitment, redeployment, and restandardization (Rescher, 1967). Moving away from "cherished personal positions and beloved hostilities may require a series of drastic events over time, recognition of a world beginning to crumble, or betrayal by those whose trust and understanding has affirmed one's personal investment in the cherished values" (Sherif, 1980:59).

The main features of the value experience (considered philosophically) are that the experience is inherently plural (we have "values"), we feel obliged to choose because values at least sometimes conflict irreconcilably and we disagree with others about them, values are experienced as occurring in hierarchies or clusters, we "naturally" experience our own values as being "objective," and we all sometimes experience "weakness of will." (Cadwallader, 1980) Or, as Bellah et al. state testily: "'Values' turn out to be the incomprehensible, rationally indefensible thing that the individual chooses when he or she has thrown off the last vestige of external influence and reached pure, contentless freedom" (1985:79-80). But then, the values which suffuse their book are self-consciously, adamantly communitarian and "old-fashioned," not individualist and "new-fashioned."

So? This is not a philosophy text (thank God!). Why this in-depth discussion of values? Can values be used to segment? Emphatically, yes. Starting at least with Vinson and Munson (1976) and Vinson, Scott, and Lamont (1977), marketers have used values as segmentation variables; however, Lee and Hensel (1990) state (I think correctly so far as academics are concerned, but incorrectly for practitioners) that twenty years of research on values in consumer research have generated a lot of articles, but little coherent result. We all know that values are important, but do not have a clear sense of how to use them (Prakash and Munson, 1985).

Personal Values and Consumer Psychology (Pitts and Woodside, 1984) contained articles on VALS, LOV (List of Values) laddering, race, ecological viewpoint, age, etc. The overwhelming conclusion one gets from reading through this volume is that there is clearly something important being discussed, researched, and described, but that no one seems to know how to extract what they are talking about and use it clearly to differentiate product offerings or do what we would today call internal marketing. Although this is not a book on using values in marketing, it is clear that the profession has dropped the ball on a behavior variable that is clear and useful; the fact that it may be difficult to define and may change (although Kamakura and Mazzon [1992] state that rank ordering of values has been stable in the United States) probably has scared marketers off. There has been some very recent research seeking to reverse this trend; Lai (1995) investigates values and consumer behavior in terms of product benefits sought.

The most commonly used instrument for values research is the venerable Rokeach Value Survey (see Table 4.2), developed by Milton Rokeach. He constructed two lists of values: eighteen "instrumental" values (those which get us to our terminal values—essentially modes of conduct) and eighteen "terminal" values—desirable states of being. An individual needs to rank order each set. This instrument has been around for over a quarter century, is well known, and has a certain inevitability about it. Nevertheless, the Survey has come under recent criticism. Braithwaite and Law (1985) tested for comprehensiveness of the thirty-six values (and found it reasonably comprehensive); however, they would have preferred a rating rather than ranking scheme on theoretical grounds. Zenzen and Hammer (1978:150) criticize more directly. They claim that the Survey fails to provide a "theory of measure-

TABLE 4.2. Rokeach's Values

Terminal	Instrumental
A comfortable life	Ambitious
An exciting life	Broadminded
A sense of accomplishment	Capable
A world of peace	Cheerful
A world of beauty	Clean
Equality	Courageous
Family security	Forgiving
Freedom	Helpful
Happiness	Honest
Inner harmony	Imaginative
Mature love	Independent
National security	Intellectual
Pleasure	Logical
Salvation	Loving
Self-espect	Obedient
Social recognition	Polite
True friendship	Responsible
Wisdom	Self-controlled

Source: Rokeach (1973).

ment, the failure to explicitly acknowledge the problem of the gap between the theoretical construct 'value' and the phenomena to be measured." The Survey has been used overseas, even in China (Wang and Rao, 1995).

Still, marketers have pressed ahead. The potential results are too powerful to ignore. As Goldberg (1976) showed twenty years ago, it is possible to predict behavior with good psychographics. There are two values-segmentation schemes available and discussed in the marketing literature. The first of these is VALS, discussed extensively below; the other is the List of Values (LOV), developed by Lynn R. Kahle (1983) and further elaborated extensively (Kahle, 1986; Kahle, Beatty, and Homer, 1986; Kahle and Kennedy, 1988; Kahle, Poulos, and Sukhdial, 1988; Beatty, Kahle, Homer, and Misra, 1985; and Beatty, Homer, and Kahle, 1988). Kahle and his co-authors concluded that VALS had serious, insurmountable problems and sought to develop an instrument that would overcome those problems and capture VALS' promise.

According to Arnold Mitchell, we are what we believe, what we dream, what we value. "For the most part, we try to mold our lives to make our beliefs and dreams come true" (1983a:3). This belief, and a lot of research that he had done in the past, led Mitchell and his team at SRI to develop VALS in the late 1970s. VALS is the intersection of Rokeach's work on values discussed above, Abraham Maslow's psychological hierarchy of needs, and David Riesman's (1950/1961) sociology. The graphical representation of the VALS typology is presented in Figure 4.2; SRI called this the "artichoke"–the two parallel but unrelated streams of segments meeting in a single stem and combining in a single top. VALS was not a true psychographic segmentation scheme, as it combined psychographics and demographics into a vivid description of the nine types it recognized. Over the next ten years, VALS became widely known in marketing circles, descriptions of it appeared in most marketing texts, and articles such as Mather (1985)–counseling marketers not to fear VALS but to accept it–and Atlas (1984)–describing the system to the general public–spread the word. Some of the ongoing SRI research (which will be discussed in some detail in Part III on implementation) appeared in public; an example of this is Ogilvy's 1986 article on the experience industry–based on Ogilvy's (1985) report for VALS subscribers.

A decided advantage that VALS had over most other psychographic segmentation schemes was the fact that it became so well known. Further, it represented an extremely good description of the population. It was not at all unusual to go to a meeting of managers, start discussing VALS, and have everyone nodding heads and saying, "Yes, those are my customers." This is not to say that VALS was problem-free; far from it. The discrepancies in segment size (nationally Belongers represented approximately 40 percent of the adult population while Emulators were only 10 percent) made it difficult for some marketers to deal with. Further, the descriptions of some segments were decidedly negative–no one would want to be described as an Emulator.

FIGURE 4.2. The VALS Typology

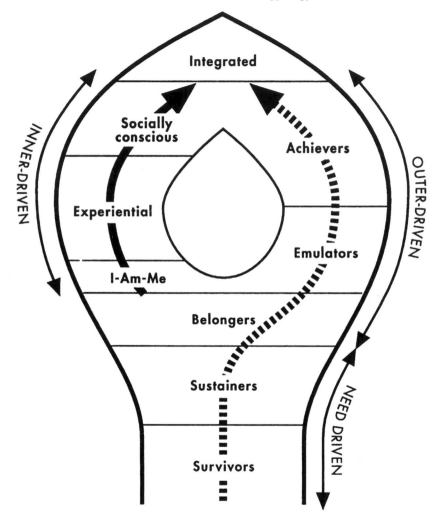

Source: Adapted from Solomon (1992), p. 502.

SRI recognized some of these problems, and the further problem that they felt–that although values were important for segmenting, the values they were using were outdated and culture-specific to the United States. In 1989, SRI introduced VALS 2 (see Figure 4.3 for a graphic representation). VALS 2 is more psychology driven rather than values driven, striving for more universal meaning (Gates, 1989). Demographics is also downplayed in VALS 2, as VALS 2 is much more of "what's going on in the customer's head" (Riche, 1989:54). Although many did not think that VALS was broken enough to need fixing (Winters, 1989), SRI responded to critics who felt that VALS was too theoretical and unpredictive (Piirto, 1990). The segments are all between 8 and 17 percent of the population; further, part of the segmentation is directly based upon consumption in over 150 product categories. How successful will VALS 2 become? It is a bit early to say, but it seems that there has to date been less coverage in the managerial and academic press than there was for VALS. Despite extensive experience with VALS, detailed in Part III below, I have not used VALS 2 very much, nor do I know anyone who has.

The LOV, according to Kahle, surpasses VALS for four reasons. First–and most important to academic researchers such as Kahle–it is in the public domain. SRI has been strongly criticized for years for not releasing any information about the construction of its measure, even after the original VALS was superseded by VALS 2.

Second, LOV collects demographic information separately from the values questions, unlike the VALS questionnaire, which combines the two. Third, the VALS questionnaire consisted of thirty-four questions; the LOV questionnaire consists of only nine. It is felt to be thus less obtrusive and people would be less reluctant to complete it. Novak and MacEvoy (1990) compared results in prediction between LOV and VALS and determined that LOV alone is not as good as VALS alone, but that adding demographic information to LOV makes this superior to using VALS by itself. Kamakura and Novak (1992) have recently looked at values segmentation again and concluded that the concept is a good idea, but the value *system* needs to be the variable used, not just the top-ranked value. Thus any good values-based questionnaire is going to be a long one.

Fourth, because the exact phrases from the survey instrument were retained in the studies using LOV (unlike the VALS process), Kahle, Beatty, and Homer (1986) have stated that communication of the research results to management is easier. It has not been my experience that Kahle's six-step process for the use of VALS (Kahle

FIGURE 4.3. The VALS 2 Typology

Source: Adapted from various SRI publications.

1985:234) has any validity. He posits that one must (1) create a consumer survey, (2) VALS classify the respondents, (3) have an account executive at the advertising agency interpret the classification results, (4) weigh the client's desires as related to the foregoing interpretation, (5) have a creative person from the agency render "these opinions" in an advertisement, which is then (6) directed back at the consumer. Kahle then states that "we have travelled a long distance from the potential consumer in the survey" at Step 1 by the end of this process (Kahle 1985:234). I would have to agree with this last statement if the technique outlined is what actually happens. What happens at most is that one creates a research instrument *with the VALS typing instrument contained therein.* There is no need for Step 2, nor are Steps 3 and 4 necessary as, in a very short period of time, everyone "speaks VALS" fluently–this is one of its very big attractions (see Case 1). Regardless of the academic validity of the typology, it is self-explanatory after attending the SRI orientation, viewing the videotapes prepared by SRI, and reading some of the VALS reports–all of which are available to subscribers. What typically happens is that one types one's market once, or at most occasionally, then deals with the "reality" that the typology shows to be present. This reduces Kahle's six steps to two: making sure that the "creative" at the agency understands VALS, and then reviewing the agency's work for VALS correctness before exposing it to the target market segments. In fact, the agency probably is more VALS-literate (or Psychographics-literate) than the client; many advertising agencies either subscribed to VALS (or now VALS 2) or developed their own proprietary psychographic segmentation schemes for their clients to use (Alsop, 1987). Ziff (1974) dealt with this problem head on: the starting point for the development of advertising (or marketing) strategy should be the segments identified through the segmentation study, assessed on the criteria of size and importance of the various targets–hardly something where the agency and the client will have to get educated about what anything means.

Thus Kahle's four advantages to LOV over VALS really boil down to two: first, it is in the public domain and thus readily accessible to all researchers, and second, it is shorter. Are these advantages worthwhile, particularly since there is no single database where the results of the LOV questionnaires used by researchers are stored? Herche has felt the need to extend the LOV methodology to develop MILOV–the Multi-Item List of Values (Herche, 1994). With what success? Although his results show that MILOV does predict consumer better than LOV, it uses more questions to do so. Therefore, we are back to nine questions for the LOV versus forty-four on MILOV! Is this progress? Kamakura and Mazzon (1991) used a value-system model to segment individuals in Brazil using basically a Rokeachean approach; by using a coherent system, rather than individual values, they have segmented more communally (which should please social critics such as Bellah et al.), but can marketers use these segments for anything but description and understanding of the groups?

How to develop a psychographic segmentation scheme? It is easier to buy one already done, but let us assume that we want one that is proprietary. V.-W. Mitchell (1994a, 1994b) has provided a road map to the process. Mitchell (1994a) is a technical discussion of the merits of factor analysis and cluster analysis, with a presentation of when to use which technique; Mitchell (1994b) presents multiple discriminant analysis in its technical complexity. Kohli and Leuthesser (1993) present similar material. The section below on perceptual mapping will deal with this in more detail.

Mitchell concludes, however, with a very nontechnical statement of the limitations of any or all of the statistical techniques mentioned: they have reliability problems, which can be troublesome because the results of the analysis "frequently look plausible" (1994b:16). However, operationalizing the segments by adding demographic data from the respondents can add to the robustness of the segmentation, adding a degree of reliability and replicability to the plausibility of the psychographic segments. (This is essentially what VALS and VALS 2 did; that is why they are not strictly speaking psychographic segmentation schemes.) The one warning I must sound about adding the demographic data is what Steven Verba, formerly of Wyse Advertising, calls the "cross-tab problem." This is a recognition that one cannot read across the bottom of one's cross tabulations and create a "model" demographic from the tables. That is, saying that our "usual" customer is a thirty-year-old female, if one tab says the usual customer is thirty years old, and another says it is female. These statements may look identical, but they are not.

Psychographics has been much maligned theoretically, usually by people grounded in statistics and psychological theory. Psychographics, according to these people, suffers from problems of reliability and validity of the measures used. Merenski (1981) answers the critics directly with the statement that, for applied marketing purposes, the usefulness of the measure is more important than its reliability or validity. Connecting Behavior A (as measured in Psychographic Profile 1) to Behavior B (as measured in Psychographic Profile 1) or Behavior A (in Profile 1) with Behavior A (in Profile 2) is relatively easy in the real world if the behaviors and profiles are drawn correctly. People's "behavior sets" are relatively coherent; if the psychographic profiles are drawn robustly, it is only at the margin that difficulty should arise–and these may be behaviors which have nothing whatever to do with marketing. This is part and parcel of a debate which has been going on in marketing for a couple of decades about reliable, valid, and useless *versus* useful but "scientifically" shaky. (This debate is frustrating to watch; see Cahill [1993] for a review of some works that have increased the frustration level–or Holbrook [1995] for an extreme statement of the position.)

Wells (1975) succinctly states why psychographic profiles are useful, even in the absence of carefully constructed measures of reliability and validity: "consider the alternatives." The alternative is usually not a profile with such carefully constructed measures; rather, it is a fallback position of crude demographics with someone's a priori statement of what "our customers" look like, or tapes from a few focus group sessions. Also, those who market to these people, who design the packages, and write the advertising copy probably do not live the lifestyle of the typical customer. Wells continues, stating that psychographic segmentations are also useful. Both are general and product-specific schemes. Although he expresses reservations about the concept (from the validity/reliability position), he again states that there are few alternatives. "Marketers know that the customers for a product or service are frequently not much alike. They know that empirical segmentation procedures hold out the possibility of new insights into how consumers may be divided into groups. . . . Given [the dilemmas], many marketers have elected to conduct and to use segmentation studies even when fully aware of the art's imperfections" (Wells, 1975:208).

Little has changed in the twenty years since Wells's article, with the exception of there being less academic reluctance to accept psychographic segmentation–at least as descriptions of market segments. As Meyer (1983) pungently states, we "all love psychographics. They make it possible to reduce large and complex populations to a few simple types which imagination can see as flesh and blood personalities instead of numerical abstractions." Of course, the reduction of complexity always comes at a price. As Dichter (1986:151) states, there are many "deeper factors, such as childhood experiences, marital power structures, and dynamic factors which have to be considered." Dichter, however, comes from the depth-psychology tradition of Vienna; one-on-one interviews of customers, while fascinating and revealing if done properly, do not do very well to classify millions of potential drinkers of beer, for example.

Goldberg (1976) tried to get around the debate on the applicability of psychographics by dealing with the product aspect of the problem. He stated that while the degree of product novelty provided a general basis for grouping different new products, a consideration of the type of product novelty ought to help categorize products, especially new products. He then hoped to be able to use these characteristics to identify relevant psychographic segments since the type of product novelty is likely to moderate consumer responses to new products. Everett Rogers, the grandfather of innovation research, has created a typology of adopter categories; the difficulty is that these categories are not psychographic segments; rather, they are "ideal conceptualizations based on observations of reality and designed to make comparisons possible" (Rogers, 1983:247). I have written on innovation before (Cahill, 1995); here I only wish to point out that an investigation of psychographic segmentation and its application to innovation and innovativeness should pay dividends. (The people at SRI thought so too; see Walling [1984] for a study of VALS types and innovation and W. Miller [1987] for a study of VALS types and creativity.)

Psychographic segmentation schemes have been very popular in the academic press as well as the marketplace. Frequently reviled by nonusers as "flashy and unnecessary," one must be reminded from time to time about the purpose behind the use of psychographics. "... [These] profiles were not designed to take the place of all other research tools. . . . Psychographic profiles should augment a total research and analysis package. . ." (Wasson, 1987:48). Wells (1975) made the same point twenty years ago in what was probably the first review essay on psychographics and psychographic techniques; the procedure should be used to enrich the marketer's understanding of the people in the target markets. Research needs continue to appear, despite the age of psychographics; Lesser and Hughes (1986) explored the generalizability of psychographics across geographic locations and found that psychographic segmentation is probably generalizable in that manner. Although Rafiq and Ahmed (1993) might flinch, creation of a psychographic profile of a firm's employees (or the use of a commercially available scheme to create such a profile) seems to be a completely appropriate use for internal marketing (see Cahill, 1996a.).

Psychographics is a tool. And like any tool, it has its limitations. Townsend (1985) lists some commonsense guidelines for its effective use:

1. Use psychographics as one technique among many. (This is the point Wasson made–cited above–and is so practical that it should not need to be repeated. But of course, it needs to be constantly reiterated.)
2. Know how you will use psychographics before you start. (Of course! Do you need to tell people what your customers are like because you don't know any? Or are you trying to accurately design a product for a particular segment? Reliability and validity issues may matter in the latter case–probably not in the former.)
3. Never stop monitoring the market. (This is true whether we are talking segmentation or selling!)

Piirto (1991) delineates eleven lessons for avoiding the pitfalls of psychographics, most of which have general applicability for most segmentation schemes–or much of marketing itself.

1. Know where you've been.
2. Extract the best from both quantitative and qualitative research.
3. Understand the underlying consumer trends.
4. Weigh the relative value of using a syndicated broad-based segmentation (such as VALS or VALS 2).
5. Use whatever techniques you're most comfortable with to get a psychographic profile of all potential customers.

6. Identify the underlying motivators.
7. When entering large foreign markets, market to the similarities, but make sure you understand and never underestimate the differences.
8. Understand the uniqueness of each local or regional market.
9. Carefully consider the sample size.
10. Make the ultimate goal of your psychographic research to identify product-specific attitudes and behaviors.
11. Know everything you can about your core customers.

I would add a twelfth lesson here, particularly true for psychographic segmentation, but true in general for all segmentation schemes. Keep testing, keep researching, keep measuring. People change, trends change, values change, everything changes. If you set your psychographics in stone in Year one, by Year six, the percentages of each segment may be radically different from what your model predicted, your media spending will be misdirected, your packaging and manufacturing will all be off, and you will not have a clue as to why things are not working. This is the point that Wells and Moore (1989) hammer on: "[Our] experiences . . . of periodic measurement have shown us time and again that periodic measurement allows us to separate the obvious truths that are true from the obvious truths that are not true. . . ."

Behavioral segmentation derives from the hypothesis that past behavior is a good indication of future behavior. For instance, those who have bought Tide detergent in the past are more likely to buy Tide detergent in the future than those who have not (always, of course, predicated on the assumption that they have been pleased with the product). Therefore, it is relatively easy to create segments of probable users—one's past and current customers—and communication schemes to reach them. Hortman et al. (1990) report a supermarket segmentation analysis based on behavior and statements made by consumers about what was important to them.

Even direct marketers, traditionally nonsegmenters—they rely rather on response modeling—can now use behavioral segmentation procedures (DeSarbo and Ramawsawmy, 1994; and see Katzenstein and Sach, 1986 for lengthy discussions of the applicability of segmentation and segmentation strategy in a direct-marketing textbook). In fact, the whole foundation of database marketing, or "integrated marketing"–the hot topic of the 1990s–is this hypothesis. Catalogue marketers have been better at using segmentation strategies than the rest of the direct marketing industry; frequently, cataloguers have more than one "brand" and segment accordingly. Thus, people in one segment might get a catalogue from Company A, while those in another segment would get a catalogue from Company B. Further, with the recent advances in printing and binding technology, firms that only send catalogues from one company can send different pages to different customers, based either on some form of segmentation (geodemographic, for instance) mentioned above–or based upon the customer's previous purchases.

Morgan, Becherer, and Richard (1979) investigated frequency of use and date of first trial as a strategic segmentation framework; they found these variables to be quite useful for identifying early heavy users of four grocery products. Values appear to contribute more to explaining heavy users' preferences than those of light users (Perkins and Reynolds, 1988).

The airlines' frequent flyer programs have been so successful that they have spawned imitators in many industries whose firms have been interested in garnering continued repeat business from loyal customers. They are examples of what has been called loyalty marketing. One author defines loyalty marketing as the "measurable process of rewarding consumer buying behavior, thereby causing long-term consumer loyalty towards a company or co-operative group of companies" (*Loyalty Marketing*, 1986:9). The rules for developing such a program are simple and the author spells them out plainly: put the customer in golden handcuffs, keep the program simple, make the rewards have value, make the customer a member of a club, target marketing to loyal customers, and establish a hierarchy of reward levels which increase customer loyalty. This list certainly describes airline and hotel frequency clubs.

However, do these programs truly build loyalty, or do they simply pay their members for repeat business? Is there a difference? After all, repeat business is repeat business, right? Wrong. Since "everyone" now has them, do they really reward loyalty? The supermarket chain I patronize in Cleveland has had a frequent buyers' club for a couple of years now, with discounts only for members, a newsletter, special contests, everything that seems to be necessary for the successful running of such a program—all of the rules mentioned above. It helps that this chain is probably a bit higher-priced than some of the others, so that the discounts given to the club members seem to represent a real attempt on management's part to lower our food bill.

Another chain, which prides itself on having the lowest prices in town recently approached its advertising agency with the charge of developing such a program—they were the last major supermarket chain in Cleveland without one. Part way into the process, one of the agency's strategic analysts asked several rather basic strategic questions: Why do you want one of these? Is this an admission (tacit, of course) that your prices are too high? Are you trying to gain market share? Gain share of customer? Attract new customers? The chain's management could not answer any of the questions—they really only wanted the program because everyone else had one and it seemed to them that they should have one, too. The loyalty marketing approach no longer works as a loyalty program in many industries because everyone has such a program. It is now simply a way to selectively reduce prices for customers (not necessarily the best customers because there is no discrimination about granting membership or retaining members who are not "frequent flyers.") Hallberg would cringe.

Part of the reason for this emphasis on past behavior is the fact that academic marketers have had a persistent problem: Attitudes research has been largely qualitative rather than quantitative and focused in strange directions. This has led to dissatisfaction with the field and the attempts to change attitudes. "Rather than change attitudes, [integrated marketing communications] seeks to change behavior. . . . We have never really been able to link attitudes to behavior" (Schultz, 1994:44). The only problem with this statement is that it is not true. Although it is true that psychologists and other behavioral scientists have had difficulties linking attitudes to behavior in laboratory settings, and that marketers have tried to deal with "Attitude Toward the Ad" and whether a positive attitude leads toward purchase of the brand, those who work with people in a social-service setting—ministers, social workers, doctors, etc.—know better. William G. Holliday, formerly the Senior Minister of Plymouth Church of Shaker Heights stated this fact bluntly in a sermon in 1993: "Not only are attitudes cultivated by people; people are cultivated by attitudes, particularly when they have developed into habits." Habits, of course, are a specific form of behavior. At the very least, attitudes represent a portion of behavior—"percentage of variance explained," to put it at its statistics worst. Attitudes form predisposing and/or precipitating factors for action (Camacho and Schmalensee, 1989).

Sherif pointedly said that an "attitude is inferred from behaviors (verbal or nonverbal), without which we can never know whether a person has an attitude" (1980:18-19). Attitudes are not static psychological entities that can be separated from the flow of action, but rather are integral parts of action. Attitude and action are linked in a continuing reciprocal process, "each generating the other in an endless chain" (Kelman, 1980:135). Kelman feels that there is *no* significant attitude change possible without action—overt behavior which "produces some change in the environment and has real-life consequences for the actor" (Kelman, 1980:119).

Chapter 5

Industrial Segmentation

According to Wind and Thomas, segmentation can be a powerful tool for industrial marketing management. "In fact, it may be the only way for some firms to survive in industries dominated by a few giant competitors" (1994:80). Segmenting other stakeholders, rather than just customers, is the true strength of industrial segmentation. This is an interesting pair of observations. First, it states that segmenting and targeting to a niche is a viable strategy alternative; one does not need to be the largest firm in an industry to survive, if one owns the niche. Second, segmenting debtholders (for example) would allow for the better placement, interest rate given, and restrictive covenant writing for a firm; if one could find bondholders who were willing to take a higher interest rate in return for fewer restrictive covenants (or vice versa), the corporate finance people could have more flexibility in dealing with their debt placement. This is a new area for marketing to make an impact on the firm's business. Other nontraditional, nonmarketing areas can benefit from segmentation. Brenner (1996) deals with using segmenting and targeting methods in shareholder relations in an attempt to find investors "whose love will last." Cahill (1996a) deals with segmentation strategies in internal marketing programs on the grounds that employees differ and that communicating with employees would be more effective if the messages were segmented and targeted.

Geography is the starting point in many industrial segmentation studies; many industrial commodities are heavy for their volume, with relatively low value per weight, and thus cannot be shipped long distances. Cement is an example of this; customers can be segmented by distance from the plant into "our guaranteed customers" because they are very close to our plant, "our potential customers" because they sit between our plant and a competitor's plant and thus we both have to try to please them, and "their customers" because they are too far from our plant to service economically.

Further, some products sell in some geographic locations and not in others. Although cross-country skis are the classic example–few in the Southern States have much use for them because of the lack of snow–some industrial goods also fit into this category. Rock salt for melting road ice is an item normally sold (at least in large quantities) only in the North. Likewise, certain admixtures for concrete do not sell in the South. When I was at Medusa Cement, I remember seeing a large bill for cement for a job in Wisconsin that started being shipped on January 2. When I asked the regional sales manager what was going on, he said that they just swept the snow off, threw some admixtures in (to keep the concrete from freezing) and pressed on. Even in the South, where temperatures rarely reach the freezing point, January is not a big month for concrete pouring–the contractors worry that it might freeze and so stop working.

The next easy segmentation variable is SIC (Standard Industrial Classification) codes. This system of numerical codes describes, digit by digit, an ever finer explanation of what a firm does, going from large industry statement (manufacturer of fabricated metal products, for example), down to an extremely specific definition (manufacturer of fabricated metal products for buildings–iron and steel). This is a good method for segmenting traditional "industrial" goods customers; so many products are intended only for a specific industry to use, or a few industries. It is easy to buy lists of firms by SIC codes, so direct marketing efforts are relatively easy. However, so many other products do not fit into this scheme: toilet paper, copy machine toner, temporary staffing services, etc. Segmenting their marketing efforts by SIC code makes little sense for firms selling these goods and services.

Behavioral traits–product usage figures–can be important. Hallberg's emphasis (mentioned near the beginning of this book) on finding the heavy users can be a key variable in business-to-business segmentation. Given the realities of many kinds of business-to-business marketing, it will be easier to find and continue to track these users than their consumer-product counterparts. Muzyka, Crittenden, and Crittenden (1986) describe a study where they segmented transit bus purchasers in two ways: behaviorally (by purchase decision similarity) and by product feature preference. Another behavioral trait that can be used to segment customers in some markets is end use versus OEM (Original Equipment Manufacturers): does the customer use the product or do they include it in something that they manufacture or do they repackage it to sell to others? This can make a difference in a firm's marketing approach to its market.

Berrigan and Finkbeiner (1992) have developed what they call a Market-Driven Business Segmentation (MBS) system which begins with customer needs. The scheme focuses on prioritizing the customer-enterprise's needs into "business strategy needs," "general business operations needs," "functional buyer needs," "management operations needs," "technology needs," "product/feature needs," and "service support needs." It then becomes possible for a firm to target its product or service offerings to the specific needs of its target market(s) and address each need separately if appropriate. This scheme is rigorous and needs a complete research program to develop the targets for a particular firm. The firm will then have to develop and maintain a large, detailed customer/prospect information system. Nevertheless, this method is not beyond the capabilities of most business-to-business firms in these days of powerful desktop computing; the only question is one of will. Further, it includes the trade-off between price and service, and other customer behavior variables which can lead to "microsegmentation" which Rangan, Moriarty, and Swartz (1992) stated was necessary in mature industrial markets–which, of course, describes most business-to-business (or consumer, for that matter) marketing situations.

Is it possible to psychographically segment groups of individuals, such as teams or companies? There have been tentative steps in this direction, made halting because of the underdeveloped nature of much of "industrial" marketing. The seminal article on this subject is by Robertson and Wind (1980), wherein the authors attempt to create "organizational psychographics" and then to use the model to explain innovativeness of organizations. Wasmer and Bruner (1991) go much further in attempting to segment employees within the service firms that share certain values and behaviors–even though they may not work together. This is done in an attempt to match rewards with behavior in a grid fashion; they state that this operational scheme of organizational psychographics is most likely to succeed in multiple-site firms, but I fail to see why such is the case. It seems to me that multiple-department firms (such as banks and hospitals, to name only two industries that consist of organizations with large numbers of employees whose site is relatively compact) might have values shared within a department that were different enough from those of other departments to segment upon, as well as employees in different departments whose values were more similar with those in other departments than they were with employees in the same department. Nevertheless, I believe that Wasmer and Bruner's point about using organizational psychographics as a means of designing marketing strategies is important. Williams and Oumlil (1983) also feel the concept of organizational psychographics to be important and useful.

Another method much endorsed in business-to-business marketing is benefit segmentation: finding out the benefits that different customers seek from the goods and services you sell to them and grouping them accordingly into segments. Supposedly, industrial buyers are smarter than consumer product buyers and they look rationally at products only for the benefits that they or their firm may derive from them. Although this type of approach forces a firm away from marketing on its product's attributes—which is not a particularly good plan—it starts from a false premise: "industrial" buyers are really no different when they enter their office than they are when they are at a grocery store. Much of the differentiation between industrial and consumer marketing is based on the "good old days" when industrial marketing meant machine tools and mainframe computers, large-ticket items with long buying cycles. The differences in mind-set between industrial marketers and consumer marketers are riveting; in what is otherwise an excellent book Jackson (1985) continually refers to "accounts" instead of customers, further depersonalizing the buyer in the industrial relationship. Martin and Hunt's (1987) development of an organization level of organizational buying behavior shows the danger in this depersonalization. Organizations, although they may have enough character and characteristics of their own to differentiate them one from another, are still composed of people; to continually refer to customers as "accounts" adds to the danger of forgetting the people at the other end. This is the essence of the story about hotels that "only a boss could love" mentioned earlier.

Bonoma and Shapiro (1983) developed a nested approach to industrial segmentation (see Figure 5.1). This approach starts with demographic variables (SIC Code, number of employees, etc.) and proceeds through several levels down to the personal characteristics of the buyers. The variables at each level really are segmentation schemes in their own right, as even a cursory investigation of the figure will show. What this approach does is segment the segments, level upon level, into ever-smaller subsegments, each with its own variable set. Complex? Very. Expensive to do? You bet.

FIGURE 5.1. The Nested Segments

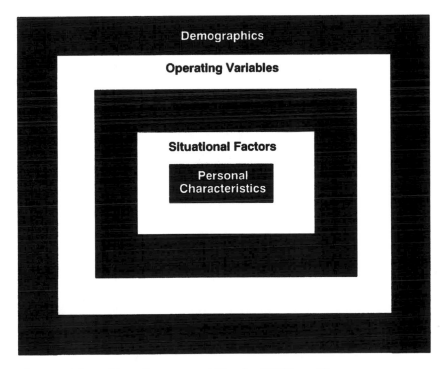

Source: Adapted from Bonoma and Shapiro (1983), p. 10.

However, Bonoma and Shapiro have enumerated two rules for using the approach. First, the nests should be investigated only deeply enough for useful segmentation to result (a good rule for any segmentation scheme, whether consumer or industrial), and second, the best way to identify economically feasible segments is through creative thinking about the customer base (1983:104). "We suggest that a marketer begin at the outside nest and work inward because data are more available and definitions clearer in the outer nest. On the other hand, the situational and personal variables of the inner nests are often the most useful" (Shapiro and Bonoma, 1983:110). Of course, always remember that the reason that a customer first bought from a firm may not be the reason the customer continues its patronage of the firm.

PART III:
TRANSLATING SEGMENTATION
IN MARKETING STRATEGY

Chapter 6

What Now?

So, now you have decided that you need to segment the market. Good decision (you hope!), but now what? This is the point at which most books, articles, and chapters on segmentation in textbooks leave you. I will not. I will take you step-by-step through some considerations that you need to think about, and some cases to show how one organization which has been a client of mine for years has used segmentation to make marketing and organizational decisions.

The first consideration is "Make or Buy?" Do you create a proprietary scheme, applicable to your firm and only your firm, which gives you a competitive edge, or do you subscribe to a syndicated service, such as VALS 2, PRIZM, or one of the other services which are available? Although the price for the syndicated services seems high, it would probably cost at least as much as the syndicated service's fee for a couple of years to develop your own scheme. If price is not a differentiating factor, what are the criteria for making a choice? Of course price would be a factor if your firm subscribed for several years, for that annual fee does add up.

First is the fact that a good syndicated service offers ongoing research and updates to its scheme. Here, I will speak from VALS experience, but much of what I have to say—but not the specifics—would be the case no matter which service we were discussing. Down through the years, either to refine their understanding of the typology or the segments or because a client had asked for specific research, SRI did many research projects for VALS which were published and made available to subscribers. There was the basic research which developed the typology (Mitchell, 1981c), work on proximities of the types, which could be used to combine two or more VALS types into single segments (Mitchell, 1981b), research on how people moved from one segment to another over time (Mitchell, 1981a), regional distribution of the VALS types (Mitchell, 1983d), the use of values in the purchase decision (Mitchell and Kimball, 1984), an update to the typology (Ploss, 1987), and more in-depth research investigating segments—the Belongers (at 40 percent of the population, the largest segment) (Mitchell, 1983b) and the Achievers (the wealthiest segment) (Mitchell, 1983c). This series of research reports represents extensive and deep understanding of the typology and how it fits American consumers.

There was also a series of research reports done specifically on the marketing implications of VALS; some of these reports are almost at a level of academic abstrusity, often leaving readers to scratch their heads and wonder what any of it might mean. Lifestyle marketing was tackled (Hampden-Turner and Carlile, 1986), the inner needs of people and how to market to them (Mitchell, 1985), how marriage works with VALS (who marries whom) and how the married dyad deals with decision making (Mitchell, 1984), how various VALS types use media and which ones they use (Kimball, 1982; Ochs, 1988). Specific industry applications also show up, such as how VALS types use direct-mail marketing (Christen and Castelli, 1986), the "Experience Industry" (Ogilvy, 1985), and travel (Skidmore and Pyszka, 1986), how attitudes and behavior toward health interact with VALS (Mills, 1988), and how VALS and an aging population interact (Gollub, 1985).

Then there were the studies that researchers did for no applied reason. Either they were attempts to answer "basic research" questions on the part of a VALS researcher, or they were attempts to use VALS to explain something deep in human behavior. There was an attempt to overlay VALS with the Myers-Briggs Type Indicator (discussed later) (Warrick, 1984). There was a deep, self-reflective look at Americans, their attitudes, ambitions, and so on (Mitchell, 1985). There were the reports on fostering creativity and how that fit in with the VALS typology (W. Miller, 1987) and the study of VALS and innovation (Wallings, 1984) mentioned earlier. But by far the most outre report of all was titled "The Emergent Paradigm" (Schwartz and Ogilvy, 1979), which spawned an academic conference on the subject (Lincoln, 1985).

Then, of course, when VALS 2 was being developed and "sold" to the VALS subscribers, reports came out beyond all of the cross-tabs, user's manuals, and other panoply that the VALS subscribers had come to expect from SRI. First was a monograph giving a report on the technical development of VALS 2 (MacEvoy, 1989), followed by an in-depth examination of "Consumer Segmentation for the 1990s" (Values and Lifestyle Program, 1989), the characteristics of the VALS 2 segments (Martin, 1989), and the use of VALS 2 in financial services (Chavez, 1989). Since that time, I am sure that there have been further reports from Menlo Park, but my client is no longer associated with the program.

Of course, there are the add-ons and spin-offs from a good syndicated segmentation provider. SRI is hooked up with PRIZM, so that you can get VALS types by ZIP+4 areas; for a direct-mail marketer, this provides the proverbial rifle armed with a silver bullet (at a high price, but if the hit rate is high, it is worth it). SRI was connected to Marshall Marketing when it was still selling VALS (and may still be with VALS 2); Marshall Marketing deals with television viewing areas. The partnership gave a television station the possibility of VALS typing its viewing area. Cleveland was typed in 1988 (Ashyk, 1988) with results that will be discussed later.

In short, using a syndicated segmentation provider gives a firm access to ongoing research and a continuing feel for its market and the changes that the market may be undergoing. Yes, this continuing research comes at a price, as do the spin-offs and tie-ins. Nevertheless, the ongoing nature of the research is a key feature of the syndicated service.

Contrast this picture with a firm that decides to go the proprietary route. The client that was the VALS subscriber left the SRI fold after a year as a VALS 2 subscriber (the details of this decision appear below). Within a couple of years of leaving VALS, he decided that he needed one of his markets explored in depth and contracted with American LIVES to do a study of the Denver, Colorado, real estate market. The principals of American LIVES were alumni of SRI, and had worked closely with Arnold Mitchell of SRI while he was there. They created a typology of the people in the Denver real estate market, consisting of five "Tribes"–and, as to be expected, the descriptions of the tribes sound quite VALS-like (see Table 6.1). My

TABLE 6.1. People/Type Descriptions

WINNERS	Highest income, education, occupation; lots of status display—want the Monument House. Winners want the biggest, most expensive of everything.
TRENDERS	Young, upward strivers, they have champagne tastes but beer budgets. They want everything the Winners have.
UPKEEPERS	Blue collar, low education. They are just getting by. They want the basics in most things.
HEARTLANDERS	Older traditionalists, they want plain-vanilla houses. They reject Winners' greed and ambition.
AUTHENTICKS	Above-average income, high education. They are against status and display. They want outdoor living room, to be close to nature.

client paid American LIVES a fee equivalent to almost two years of VALS fees for the study. He was quite happy with the results, for they fit what people in the real estate market across the country see as the kinds of people who come in to their offices to buy and sell houses. But the survey was done in 1991 and is now getting rather dated; my client does not want to spend the money again to update the study, nor has he ever spent the money to run a similar study in any of the other markets he serves.

This is one problem with a proprietary classification scheme. With no other subscribers, all of the costs of development and ongoing research must be born by the single firm, and these costs are not trivial. Another negative aspect needs to be explored. VALS and VALS 2 (and LOV and PRIZM, etc.) work with any product and any city; the American LIVES scheme does not. It is a scheme designed to type houses and the people who buy and sell them. Despite the fact that one's house is one's biggest single purchase, it is not the only purchase one makes.

The public nature of houses, however, is not confined to the obvious—the outside appearance of the house. The contents of the house are also critical. The possessions represent the inward being of the owner. Although one may have little control over that which is encountered outside the house–given zoning codes and peer pressures–household objects are chosen and could be discarded if they cause too much conflict with oneself. The configurations of material possessions in suites serve to locate us in terms of class, status, and social position; these categorical evaluations give rise to impressions of the owner's personal qualities and attributes (see Nasar, 1988a). "Some evidence tentatively suggests that these impressions based on relative wealth are consensual" and widely shared (Dittmar, 1992:160). The effects are social, "but the cues on the basis of which the social situations are judged are environmental–the size of the room, its location, its furnishings. . . . They all communicate identity, status, and the like, and through this they establish a context and define a situation" (Rapoport, 1982:56).

These things do not exist in isolation, but rather in sets, what Grant McCracken (1988:120) has called "Diderot Unities"–highly consistent complements of consumer goods. These unities are groups of goods that go together, "in large part because their symbolic properties bring them together. It is the cultural, meaningful aspect of goods that help to give them their secret harmonies" (McCracken, 1988:121). Although McCracken named the effect, it is one which people have known about intuitively for decades, if not centuries. "The more rich Italians spent for buildings [in the fourteenth and fifteenth centuries], the more they found themselves spending for the furnishing of these places, both domestic and ecclesiastical; hence, their investment in architecture had a multiplier effect in the expansion of their world of goods" (Goldthwaite, 1993:62). This is the social psychology of possessions. ". . . [The] symbolic meanings of possessions and wealth are an integral feature of expressing one's own identity and perceiving the identity of others . . . has to lead to the proposition that material possessions have profound significance for the social psychological reality of everyday life" (Dittmar, 1992:205). It is part of what drives style and fashion, that once one has introduced a new chair into a room, the rest of the furniture no longer looks right. So long as we are discussing furniture intended for use, in public areas of the house intended for viewing by others, it is probable that the introduction of that chair would lead to the purchase of additional new furniture for the room. If, however, we are discussing the introduction of a new chair into one's private study, an inner sanctum, it is exceedingly improbable that the introduction of that chair will lead to any such set of additional purchases.

> The reasons people give for cherishing their household possessions reveal a picture of the meaning of life for urban Americans that is in some respects familiar, but in others, strikingly unexpected in its detail. We get a sense of a life in which immediate experience, a search for enjoyment, is important. At the same time, one feels an almost equally strong desire to remember the good times of the past and especially to preserve the relationships experienced with people very close to oneself. This search for meaning seems to proceed in an almost complete vacuum of formal goals and values. This does not mean that goals and values are absent. They are often implicit in the other reasons about which respondents talk. But none of the great spiritual and ideological systems that are supposed to have moved people in the past have left objective traces in the homes of these Americans nor has a new configuration as yet taken their place (Csikszentmihalyi and Rochberg-Halton, 1981:87).

This concern is probably stronger in the United States than in most other societies.

> The impression of a society of consumers raised images of breaking down the isolation of people. Shared goods meant having more in common; therefore, a scattered society still could be close, even if it meant that strangers could hide behind the facade of their things. People could create status differences not through their character, but through their accumulation of luxuries. . . . The consumer system reached across the land, advancing in apparent defiance of the land. . . . Texts were more important in a consumer system, since people who were increasingly strangers to one another relied on signs to communicate. . . . People on the move needed more signs to guide them through the changing landscape and their changing lives [than those in rooted societies] (Bronner, 1989:51).

Further, since people are social beings, we cannot explain the demand for and the use of goods and services by looking solely at the actual physical properties of goods and services. "Man needs goods for communicating with others and for making sense of what is going on around him." Thus the need to communicate is tied up in the need to have physical goods. Communication can only be formed in a "structured system of meanings. . . . [One's] overriding objective as a consumer . . . is a concern for information about the changing cultural scene" (Douglas and Isherwood, 1979:95).

Because of the "Diderot Unity" nature of one's possessions, it should be as easy to type somebody from what they own as from a paper-and-pencil instrument such as the VALS questionnaire. That is, if you wear a Rolex watch, drive a BMW, and wear an Armani suit, chances are you are an Achiever (in VALS terms). SRI produced a film where they went to a Belonger couple, an Achiever couple, and a Societally Conscious couple and asked them to bring out some products that were important in their lives and talk about them (SRI, 1989). They also produced a film about all of the types, showing one or two products the people bought and things that the people did–a good orientation to VALS (SRI, 1983). The films were so "typecast" as to be almost caricature. The Societally Conscious couple (she was a Unitarian minister, he a lawyer for Legal Aid) talked about the gallon jug of olive oil they bought direct from "the grower down the road"–with no label. The Belonger couple used Colgate toothpaste; when asked if she had ever used a pump, the wife said she had, but "it didn't do anything for me." I have shown this tape to people, blocking out the explanation of what type they were and asked VALS-literate individuals to identify them by their array of products–with 100 percent accuracy.

A proprietary segmentation scheme–particularly one designed for a single product or service like my client's American LIVES segmentation scheme–will have a great deal of difficulty dealing with the Diderot Unity nature of consumption. It will prove difficult to go backwards from products to type. Many years ago, while the client was a VALS subscriber, we had discussed the possibility of using an electronic kiosk he had developed which showed pictures of houses for sale to do a "backwards VALS typing." If we could figure out which types lived in what kinds of houses, we could then figure out what VALS type a person was, based on the first few houses he or she asked to have saved by the kiosk for further review; then, the computer program would only show them the houses which that VALS type should be interested in. This idea came to nought (see Cahill, 1990, and Verba and Cahill, 1993 for the story of InfoVision), but the concept is intriguing.

The next question about using segmentation strategies and creating typologies of customers that needs to be answered, whether the segments in the typology bear numbers or names which may be patronizing or pretentious, is what do the customers think of such an approach? Typologies in the social sciences in general and marketing in particular have a long and distinguished career. Hardly an issue of the *Journal of Marketing* seems to pass without another study by an academic researcher creating yet another typology along some set of criteria. Practitioners also have created numerous, usually proprietary, typologies to describe various segments of the population.

No one seems to have asked what the customer thinks about all of this, or at least published the results of such a survey. Marketing executives and academics are familiar with the existence of typologies and segmentation schemes and their use; are customers familiar with them? Would they resent being pigeonholed by marketers if they found out? This is an important series of questions because typologies can be an important method of theory building, not just a descriptive tool. Doty and Glick state that typologies are not simply "sloppy classification system[s]." Properly constructed, they are "complex theoretical statements that should be subjected to quantitative modeling and rigorous empirical testing" (Doty and Glick (1994:231). They state the following guidelines to improve the development of typologies that are theory building:

1. Typological theorists should make explicit their grand theoretical assertion(s).
2. Typologies must define completely the set of ideal types.
3. Typologies must provide complete descriptions of each ideal type using the same set of dimensions.

4. Typological theories should explicitly state the assumptions about the theoretical importance of each construct used to describe the ideal types.
5. Typological theories must be tested with conceptual and analytical models that are consistent with the theory (Doty and Glick, 1994:246-247).

These are not trivial questions and considerations. I had a client who was vitally interested in the use of typologies as theory building and the reaction of consumers if they found out that they were being "pigeonholed." Douthit Communications felt impelled to understand whether their customers' customers would be able to use a segmentation scheme or if they would be offended if Douthit's customers—real estate firms—used the scheme on them.

Douthit Communications decided to retain Gallup Applied Science to research their *Homes Illustrated* magazines. Gallup was retained to perform EYE-TRAC® research on the magazines to determine specifically how people viewed the advertisements contained in them. As part of the exercise, however, there would be opportunities to ask the EYE-TRAC® respondents some open-ended questions; we wished to directly confront the issue of the subjects' attitudes toward being "people typed."

The EYE-TRAC® test was conducted in Waltham, Massachusetts, in August 1994. Prospective home buyers were prerecruited and screened by telephone using only two sampling criteria: intent to buy a house within the next five years and an age range between thirty and forty-nine years. Purchase intention is clearly necessary for a sample which is to look at a house-for-sale magazine (but not to discuss typologies). The age range criterion had a twofold purpose: the bottom of the range was added to keep the sample reasonably "clean" for house-buying purposes, and the upper age limit was dictated by equipment needs of the EYE-TRAC® apparatus.

Upon arrival at the site, study participants were asked to complete a short self-administered questionnaire designed to obtain information about intent to buy a house, description of the individual's current and ideal house, where they were in the house-buying process, and attitudes toward real estate advertisements. After completing this questionnaire, the subjects were led into the room with the

EYE-TRAC® apparatus. After completing the EYE-TRAC® portion of the study, an exit interview was administered which involved several questions, including those specifically about their reaction to typologies and being pigeonholed.

Prior to performing the research, my client and I had hypothesized that the subjects would be interested in the two typologies, but that they would be offended by the use of the people typology in an applied marketing case–a real estate agent's eyeing them over, trying to figure out which type they were in order to sell them a specific house.

The subjects were then told to keep the card with the people types and asked: "The people groups or categorizations which you have on this card are used by many companies to help them describe the people who use or buy their products or services. As a prospective home buyer, how useful do you think it is to categorize people in the real estate market in this manner?" They were then given a 4-point Likert scale from Very Useful through Not At All Useful. The responses by subject are: 10 percent said it would be very useful, 49 percent said somewhat useful, 14 percent said not very useful, and 24 percent said not at all useful. It is possible that consumers may not mind marketers' using a typology to categorize them.

The research described above is, of course, full of caveats and the need for further research. Beyond the usual expressions of small sample size (n = 30), all from one geographical area (Greater Boston), a small age range (thirty to forty-nine), one must include the fact that the question was asked in only one product category and the results for "housing" may not carry over to "shirts." Further, some of the results do not fit well with the large survey undertaken in the Denver market which created the two typologies (American LIVES, 1991) , particularly with respect to the percentages of individuals in each of the types. The Denver study clustered the respondents based upon a survey instrument; the EYE-TRAC® study allowed people to be self-identified into the types with only sketchy descriptions of the types. This fact may account for a large portion of the difference between Denver and Waltham; however, it is possible that the types found in Denver may not be generalizable. Further, given the fact that I have not found any references where a typology was disclosed starkly to consumers, it is possible that the concept of doing so is flawed from the start.

Nevertheless, the result mentioned above is tantalizing. It is possible that the American public will not resent being pigeonholed or stereotyped, if they can see a positive benefit to them from being placed in a typology. The benefit may need to be either economic, or it may need to be an efficiency benefit—a "time saving." The process of buying and selling a house is so awful for most people that anything that can be done to simplify and speed up the process seems to be welcomed. I would expect that there are other goods and services where this might be the case. I know that for some people the speed of going though a catalog and ordering over the telephone is a big benefit to catalog buying; this aspect of time pressure, discussed thoroughly in Chapter 4, is an obvious segmentation variable. If this is the case, it would behoove marketers not only to develop typologies (or use syndicated ones), but to communicate the fact that they are using them and why they are using them with their customers as a direct, quantifiable benefit for them.

Chapter 7

Perceptual Mapping

What is perceptual mapping? In its marketing application, the term means a technique used to graphically represent the position of a particular offering in terms of all the other offerings in a specific category of products or services. There are generally two goals in mind when managers have perceptual maps drawn. The first is to determine where the offering is positioned with respect to the competitive offerings. The second is to help identify product or service attributes which are important to customers and which can be used to differentiate one company's offering from the others in the category. No matter how important a particular attribute may be in the customer's mind, unless the customer perceives differences across offerings, then that attribute will not be influential in customer's decisions when faced with choosing among alternatives. Frequently, the attributes which customers find important are latent, and often unobservable (or, usually, are deemed unimportant) by management; perceptual mapping helps in the essential task of uncovering these latent dimensions and making them and their importance more apparent to all concerned.

Why do perceptual mapping? Very simply, because it is often easier for people to *see and understand* relationships when they are presented graphically rather than in columns of figures or in long verbal descriptions. The various techniques of perceptual mapping which will be presented later in this chapter all deliver a graphic map of the various attributes, locating in space the different offerings already in the marketplace with relation to each other and with relation to the various attributes uncovered by quantitative surveying of customers and potential customers. The numbers used to create the maps can be presented to managers in tabular form, but they are not easy to interpret in that form. When they are presented to managers in the form of a graph or map, their interpretation is made easier; in fact, the interpretation often becomes so obvious that decisions can be made very quickly and with little discussion. Schmalensee and Thisse (1986) state that such mapping is usually done early in a new product development process; however, there is no reason to discontinue doing such maps after the product is introduced.

Perceptual mapping is not a technique which has direct applicability to segmentation, for the maps are of product or service attributes and not customers or prospects. Nevertheless, they are important to designing segments and approaches for targeting the segments, for each segment must, by necessity, have a differing perceptual map from other segments with regard to the importance of various attributes, or the segments may not be correctly designed.

What one hopes to derive from the process of perceptual mapping is that the gaps in the current offerings in a market will become apparent. Figure 7.1 shows a conjectural map of various orchestras and chamber music groups in Cleveland, mapped along the dimensions of Amateur/Professional, and "Daringness of music programmed"—a measure of how much unfamiliar or new music that group presents. If one wanted to launch another group, some gaps in the current offerings are apparent. First, Apollo's Fire jumps out from the figure as filling a previous gap; it is a professional chamber group performing mostly Baroque music and there is nothing else in its niche. Are there other gaps?

Try Figure 7.2, a map on the Amateur/Professional dimension, but search along another dimension—cost of tickets—which consumers would undoubtedly find important and which would give a new entrant a marketable differentiation. The Trinity Orchestra/Chamber Players perform primarily during a "brownbag" series of concerts, all of which are free and open to the public at noon in a near-downtown Episcopal Cathedral. In Figure 7.1, you can see that these concerts are not "daring," differentiating themselves from several similar small orchestras in the area only by being professional; many of the members of this group are members of the Akron Symphony or Canton Symphony—professional ensembles in smaller cities near Cleveland. When the dimension of ticket price is used

FIGURE 7.1. Hypothetical Perceptual Map of Selected Cleveland Area Orchestras and Chamber Groups

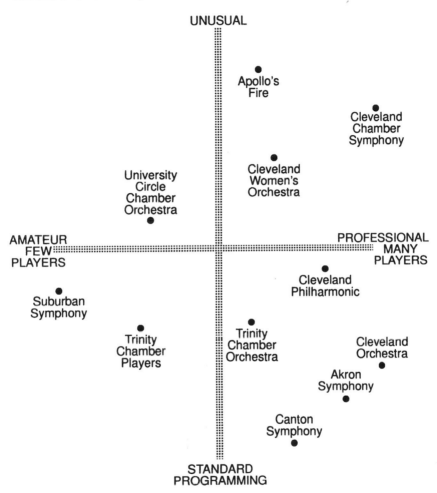

Source: From Cahill (1995), p. 33.

instead of "daringness," this group's uniqueness becomes quickly evident. As a frequent attendee at their concerts, I can also testify to the power of that free admission; when they charge even a nominal amount for a concert, attendance plummets. These maps would

FIGURE 7.2. Hypothetical Perceptual Map of Selected Cleveland Area Orchestras and Chamber Groups

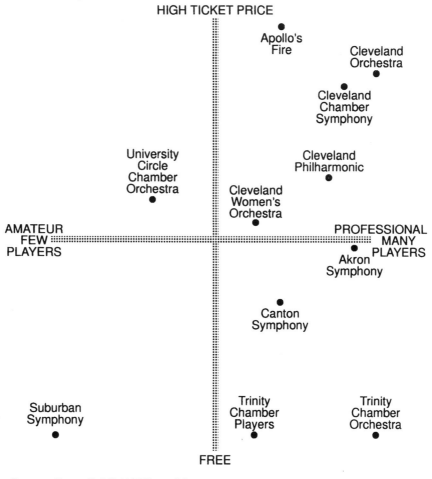

Source: From Cahill (1995), p. 34.

make it relatively easy for decision makers to start crafting a new group's offering so as not to compete head-on with other, more established, musical organizations in town.

There have not been many examples in the published literature of perceptual maps for services. One of the few was presented by

Horne, McDonald, and Williams (1986). The authors randomly contacted an entire area code for respondents to evaluate forty-three services on twenty-five different dimensions, ranging from personnel versus equipment performing the service, social risk, financial risk, to amount of face-to-face contact. A rather complete map was prepared based upon the results. Sisodia (1993) did a study of how brokerage firms and financial institutions select one another. Two multidimensional scaling techniques were used to develop perceptual maps of clusters of firms selling clusters of attributes.

So much for the explanation of why one should do perceptual mapping. How does one go about doing the job? There are three basic techniques which I will discuss in the next section: factor analysis, discriminant analysis, and multidimensional scaling. Each has its uses–and advocates. Kohli and Leuthesser (1993) in a recent article aimed directly at managers, outlined these three techniques and compared their strengths and weaknesses and described when to use which. I strongly recommend that the actual design of the surveys and preparation of the perceptual maps themselves be done by researchers who are trained in the techniques, although software designed to aid in these techniques is becoming more accessible all the time.

Techniques

Factor Analysis is essentially a data reduction technique in which the objective is to represent the original assembly of a large number of attributes in terms of a (one hopes much) smaller number of underlying dimensions or factors. After the factors have been identified, the brands' ratings on these factors are used to position the brands in perceptual space. The first step is to produce "factor loadings," which is roughly analogous to a set of correlation statistics. Each factor loading is a measure of the importance of the variable in measuring each factor. The "explanation of variance" in the variable is displayed numerically in the Factor-Loading Table as a single statistic–analogous to the R in multiple regressions. After all of this statistical work is completed, it is possible to take the data points and plot them into a graph, thus showing graphically where each of the offerings lies. It is a powerful tool.

Cluster analysis may be used to identify offerings that are similar along some criteria. As a technique, it is less sophisticated than factor analysis, but it is also easier to perform. The purpose of cluster analysis is to group offerings into a small number of mutually exclusive groups with quite similar characteristics so that they may be discussed as if they were a single offering. It is a technique that is frequently employed in doing market segmentation studies.

Discriminant analysis is also used to reduce the number of attributes to a smaller number of underlying dimensions. However, discriminant analysis focuses on the attributes that show differences between offerings. Discriminant analysis tends to ignore attribute ratings that show large variations within offerings and focuses instead on attribute ratings which show large variations between offerings (or, to put it another way, from one respondent to another). A major difference in the method of presentation is that in the perceptual maps prepared from discriminant analysis it is possible to assess how strong the agreement among respondents on one factor is in relation to other factors.

In their comparison of factor analysis and discriminant analysis, Kohli and Leuthesser (1993:18) give a road map of when to use discriminant and when to use factor analysis. Discriminant analysis should be preferred when there are objective dimensions to measure; the two techniques can be used complementarily to highlight substantial differences in agreement among consumers; and factor analysis should be preferred when there are few offerings in a category. Multidimensional Scaling (MDS) maps offerings spatially, so that their relative position in the mapped space reflects the degree of perceived similarity between them. Respondents evaluate–either in rank order or rate–the offerings in pairs, judging the overall similarity between the paired offerings. Unlike either factor analysis or discriminant analysis, MDS asks respondents to rate offerings on overall similarity, not individual attributes.

Kohli and Leuthesser (1993:15-16) mention some considerations in making the decision whether to use MDS or factor analysis or discriminant analysis. First, MDS works better the larger the number of offerings available for respondents; in markets where there are only a few offerings (such as the Cleveland newspaper market), MDS loses power. Second, and offsetting this desirability of large numbers of offerings, is the fact that the larger the number of offerings, the more complex the rating or rank ordering job that faces respondents. This calls into question some of the real-world validity of the results. Third, MDS requires only similarity judgments for the pairings; therefore, it is not necessary to do prior research to determine which product or service attributes are important in consumer choice. Thus, when it is not clear that the relevant attributes can be specified for respondents, Kohli and Leuthesser recommend using MDS.

In discussions with several market researchers about why these techniques are not used more frequently, two major points arose. First, as I reviewed the literature on perceptual mapping, I noticed that much of the academic work was done in the late 1970s and early 1980s (see Cooper, 1983, for a review), and that relatively little has been done more recently—although these techniques still appear in marketing research textbooks. Since there has been relatively little recent academic interest, it stands to reason that the techniques have not been taught much. Cooper's paper cited 158 academic articles, papers, book chapters, and books relating only to MDS and its impact on marketing subjects spanning the field, including product planning, market structure analysis, market segmentation, pricing, branding, channels of distribution, personal selling, and advertising—but the article is now a decade old.

There is one recent article that offers some exciting applications of what a practitioner would call "quick and dirty" mapping. Steven Shugan (1987) estimated brand positions by regression of aggregate sales data based upon output from supermarket scanners. He concluded that managers can derive a perceptual map, albeit not a map with a great deal of richness of raw information, from observed choice behavior as delivered by supermarket scanners in such abundance. Managers can then study the direct effect of both a brand's price and its positioning on sales. Unfortunately, "pure" services cannot be handled in such a manner because there is no bar-coded product to run through the scanner, but the product portion of a service—such as McDonald's hamburgers or Domino's pizza—certainly could be. Nevertheless, Shugan's article is interesting in continuing to use an old technique.

Second, there seem to be a few research firms that use these techniques as rather standard tools in their kit, but most firms do not use them at all. The firms that do use the techniques tend to use them a lot. Wyse Advertising in Cleveland has long been an avid practitioner of perceptual mapping, primarily MDS. Their favorite computer program for analysis is MDPREF, since it is an internal form of analysis where only the original data are used in interpretation, whereas in some other techniques, additional information is employed (Kowalysko, n.d. a and b). Although there are arguments for one program over another, they are not important here. What is important is that the tools are readily available and understood by most marketing PhDs, so that finding a researcher to produce and interpret the perceptual maps should not be a problem in most communities in the United States.

Chapter 8

Marketing Communications

The next important question to answer is "How do we communicate with our market?"—how to communicate with the segments we have created. It makes little or no sense to segment a market by demographics, geographics, psychographics, or tea leaves and then to communicate with the segments as if they were all alike. Therefore, a good communications strategy needs to segment the communications in a way that the appropriate message for each segment is communicated to that segment appropriately, with as little "spillover" to another segment as possible.

Fortunately, such a technique is readily available in the Myers-Briggs Type Indicator (MBTI). Strongly grounded, not in Freudian psychology, but in the work of Carl Jung, the MBTI has been around for decades (Myers and McCaulley, 1985). It is quite possible that you have not heard of it both because it is only now gaining academic respectability (because of its lack of Freudian base) and the fact that its strongest supporters have for years been educators.

The MBTI, a fairly long (126 items) instrument, separates people into "Types" along four dimensions: Perception (Sensing or Intuition); Judgment (Thinking or Feeling); Attitude (Extraversion or Introversion); and Orientation to the Outer World (Judgment or Perception). There is not a hint in either Jungian theory or in the MBTI itself that one type is "better" than another; no "therapist" will try to "cure" you of your type. This is one of the appeals of type theory as opposed to Freudian psychology: it deals with healthy people. After responding to the instrument, people are then classified into one of sixteen types based upon which of the items in each dimension is dominant (See Figure 8.1); for instance, my Type is INTJ: I am an Introvert (as defined by Jung–I also am introverted according to the normal definition, but the two do not necessarily go together); I perceive things Intuitively (with my brain and not with my hands–I am not an experimenter); my judgments are based on internal thinking, not concern with how others feel; and my orientation to the outer world is judgment-based.

Great! Now what? There has been a lot written on MBTI, describing the sixteen Types, how Type connects with temperament, what it all means, etc. There is an national association–the Association for Psychological Type –which publishes material and sponsors a biennial scholarly conference complete with papers on many subjects connected with type theory and practice. There are dozens of

FIGURE 8.1. The Sixteen Types

		SENSING TYPES		INTUITIVE TYPES			
		WITH THINKING	WITH FEELING	WITH FEELING	WITH THINKING		
INTROVERTS	JUDGING	**ISTJ**	**ISFJ**	**INFJ**	**INTJ**	JUDGING	INTROVERTS
	PERCEPTIVE	**ISTP**	**ISFP**	**INFP**	**INTP**	PERCEPTIVE	
EXTROVERTS	PERCEPTIVE	**ESTP**	**ESFP**	**ENFP**	**ENTP**	PERCEPTIVE	EXTROVERTS
	JUDGING	**ESTJ**	**ESFJ**	**ENFJ**	**ENTJ**	JUDGING	

books on the subject in general; probably the best way into the older material is through Myers (1980). One can get into this as deeply as one wants; however, my goal here is to deal with the use of the MBTI as a tool for improving communications.

Table 8.1 outlines the preferred methods of communication along each of the dimensions (interestingly, not by the sixteen Types). It is fairly clear that communicating to people is not simple. Given the fact that most firms will sell goods or services to people from each of the types, it becomes apparent that a communication strategy must be developed that approaches talking with each group quite differently. Yeakley (1982) warns against accepting too quickly the hypothesis that type similarity equals easier and better communications.

This is true even if the people you want to talk to fall into the same group along other dimensions or in other segmentation schemes. Several years ago, DECOY, Inc. (for details about this firm, see Case 1 in the appendix) retained National Market Measures, a Cleveland market research firm, to do focus groups for three VALS groups on how they reacted to different house styles (this research will be discussed in detail a bit later). A focus group was convened for Achievers, Belongers, and the two Inner-Directed groups. The latter two groups were successful and provided quite a great deal of information. The Achiever group was a total flop; according to the moderator, it was the most difficult group to run that she had ever encountered, because they simply would not follow up with each other and tended to answer in two- or three-word sentences. We sent the tape of this group out to SRI for their comments. The analyst called me immediately, chuckling. "You ran into a bad MBTI pattern," was his comment, "run the group again." We did, with much more success. Same psychographic profile, different communication pattern.

Yeakley (1983:22-23) presents four listening styles that have tremendous importance for designing communications strategies. Listening in the sensing style means interpreting at a practical level and asking such questions as: What is the speaker saying? How should the words be decoded? How should the message be perceived? Listening in the intuitive style means understanding at a much deeper level than the sensing style and asking such questions as: What does the speaker really mean? What are the assumptions

TABLE 8.1. Preferred Methods of Communication

Extroversion	Introversion
Communicate energy and enthusiasm	Keep energy and enthusiasm inside
Respond quickly	Like to think before responding
Focus of talk is on people and things	Focus is on internal ideas and thoughts
Need to moderate expression	Need to be drawn out
Seek to communicate in groups	Seek to communicate one-to-one
Prefer face-to-face to written	Prefer written to face-to-face
Sensing	**Intuition**
Like evidence presented first	Like global schemes presented first
Want practical applications	Want possible future challenges discussed
Rely on direct experience	Rely on insights and imagination
Use orderly step-by-step approach in presentations	Use round-about approach in presentations
Follow agenda in meetings	Bypass agenda in meetings
Refer to specific examples	Refer to general concepts
Thinking	**Feeling**
Prefer to be brief and concise	Prefer to be sociable and friendly
Want the pros and cons listed	Want to know how alternatives affect people
Convinced by cool impersonal reasoning	Convinced by personal information
Present goals and objectives first	Present points of agreement first
Consider emotions and feelings as data to weigh	Consider logic and objectivity as data to value
Seek involvement with tasks in meetings	Seek involvement with people in meetings
Judgment	**Perception**
Want to discuss schedules and timetables	Want to discuss schedules but are uncomfortable with deadlines
Dislike surprises	Enjoy surprises
Expect others to follow through	Expect others to adapt to situational requirements
State positions and decisions clearly	Present their views as tentative and modifiable
Communicate results and achievements	Communicate options and opportunities
Talk of purpose and direction	Talk of autonomy and flexibility
Focus on task to be done	Focus on process to be appreciated

Source: Pridgen (1988), p. 30.

underlying the message? What are the message's implications? What are the possibilities suggested by the message? Listening in the thinking style means analyzing and organizing while asking such questions as: What is the message's structure? What is its central idea? What are its main points and subpoints and how are they related? Is there adequate evidence to justify each claim? Is the reasoning logical? Are the claims true or false? Listening in the feeling style means evaluating and appreciating while asking such questions as: What values are suggested by the message? Should these values be accepted or rejected? How do I feel about the message? How do I feel about the speaker? The true significance of Yeakley's article is that most of us use different listening styles at different times; we may tend to listen in the thinking style, but we can and do listen in other styles. It is therefore incumbent upon those designing communications strategies and executions to be aware of this fact and deal with it, making it possible for us either to stay in our preferred style or go to another listening style if it is evidently appropriate for the particular message.

McBride and Cline (1989) report on a campaign designed by students at Southwest Texas State University for Apple Computer (at Apple's request). The campus campaign was to increase awareness of the Apple Macintosh's benefits, increase knowledge of the Apple Purchase Program, and announce Apple's new student-financing program. The students utilized several type-discovering techniques to infer the dominant types on campus and designed their campaign to match those types. The campaign was very successful, a fact which the authors attribute mostly to the fact that the students were able to match the communications approach of the advertising campaign with the psychological types on campus.

How to discover your customers' Types? Giving the MBTI to a sample of customers is the obvious choice; it is not difficult or expensive to administer—less than $5.00 per survey plus the fee for the psychologist to administer it if no one in your firm is so licensed (Consulting Psychologists Press is the source for the instrument). However, some customers would possibly object to the test and being typed—even though the MBTI, not being a therapy-based instrument, treats all the types as equally valid and no one type is "better" than any other. It is possible to infer people's types from their overt behavior; this technique was developed by educators whose students were too young to take the test–which is strictly for adults (Lawrence, 1982). Although not all of the checklists in Table 8.2 have been field tested, they do seem to work; if one is familiar with type theory and practice, of course, they would work better. And, of course, remember that these items were designed for teachers to use; consumers' behavior will be different and the consumer research will be looking for different traits.

After reading Tables 8.1 and 8.2, the question inevitably arises as to the possibility of getting to a person's MBTI "backwards"–that is, are people in a group more likely to have the same type? To a certain extent, the answer is yes. McDaid, McCaulley, and Kainz's work (1986) represents an attempt to digest the results of the thousands of people who have taken the MBTI down through the years. The total Center for Psychological Type data bank population of MBTI records consists of 232,557 records for the years 1971-1984; the distribution of types ranges from a low of ESTP (3.08 percent) to a high of ENFP (10.52 percent) of the population. There were 59,784 records with usable occupational codes and the Atlas attempts to deal with these. For instance, Accountants (N = 427) are ISTJ (20.14 percent–the next highest category is ESTJ with 12.41 percent) ; almost half of CPAs (N = 494) fall into these two categories–26.72 percent and 19.23 percent respectively; marketing personnel (N = 83) are ENTJ (15.66 percent) and ENTP (13.25 percent), with reasonably similar concentrations of ESTP, ENFP, and ESTJ, all over 9 percent; salesworkers (N = 1750) were ESTJ (12.69 percent), ENFP (11.03 percent), and ESFJ (10.06 percent). Further, Brock and Demarest (1989) report a method for using type theory and observation of client's behavior to infer their type in an effort to sell better to each type; Twining (1990) presents another approach to sales training.

SRI did some work about VALS type and MBTI type in an attempt to link the two (Warrick, 1984); there has been some similar research with the MBTI and LOV (McIntyre, Claxton, and Jones, 1994). Key findings of that research were that the outer-directed VALS types (Belongers and Achievers in particular) were more extraversion-oriented, while the inner-directed VALS types (Societally Conscious and Experiential in particular) were more Introver-

TABLE 8.2. Observation of Type Inferences

If your employee is an EXTROVERT, it is likely that he or she:

- Chooses to work with a group
- Plunges into new experiences
- Is relaxed and self-confident
- Is interested in others and their doings
- Readily offers opinions
- Shares personal experiences
- Wants to experience things so as to understand them
- Asks questions to check on the expectations of the group or leader
- Has a relatively short attention span
- Dislikes complicated procedures and gets impatient with slow jobs
- Acts quickly, often without thinking
- Likes to work by trial and error

If your employee is an INTROVERT, it is likely that he or she:

- Likes to work alone
- Holds back from new experiences
- Chooses written assignments
- Pauses before answering and shows discomfort with spontaneous questioning
- Asks questions to understand something before attempting to do it
- Seems "deep"
- Is intense
- Prefers setting own standards when possible
- Likes quiet space in which to work
- Works intently on the task at hand
- Dislikes interruptions
- May spend too much time in thought and neglect to get started

If your employee prefers SENSING, it is likely that he or she:

- Is realistic and practical
- Is more observant than imaginative
- Enjoys owning things and making them work
- Prefers memorizing to finding reasons
- Learns best from an orderly sequence of details
- Is interested in facts
- Keeps accurate track of details; is a listmaker
- Is patient
- Is good at precise work
- Likes to know the "right way" to solve problems
- Likes an established routine
- Works steadily, not in fits and starts
- Is impatient or frustrated with complicated situations

TABLE 8.2 *(continued)*

If your employee prefers INTUITION, it is likely that he or she:

- Seems to like something new all the time
- Is more imaginative than observant
- Attends more to the concept than the details
- Becomes restless and impatient with routine
- Is an initiator, innovator
- Sees possibilities that others miss
- Is quick with finding solutions
- Doesn't always hear you out; anticipates your words
- Enjoys learning a new skill more than using it
- Works in bursts of energy with slack periods between
- Jumps to conclusions, makes factual errors
- Finds reading easy

If your employee prefers THINKING, it is likely that he or she:

- Wants logical reasons before accepting new ideas
- Tries to be fair
- Is impersonal and objective
- Finds ideas and things more interesting than people
- Is brief and businesslike
- Takes facts, theories, and the discovery of truth very seriously
- Treats emotional relationships and ideals casually
- Contributes intellectual criticism
- Exposes wrongs in the habits and beliefs of others
- Is offended by illogic
- Holds firmly to a policy or conviction
- Hurts other people's feelings without knowing it
- Has a low need for harmony
- Is upset by injustice

If your employee prefers FEELING, it is likely that he or she:

- Is personable
- Is more interested in people than things
- Is more tactful than truthful
- Is likely to agree with others in the group
- Thinks as others think, believing them to be probably right
- Finds it difficult to be brief and businesslike
- Takes emotional relationships and ideals very seriously
- Is offended by a lack of personal consideration in others
- Is motivated by others
- May comply or conform to avoid disharmony
- Permits feelings to override logic

- Forecasts how others will feel
- Arouses enthusiasm
- Is upset by conflict, values harmony
- Dislikes telling people unpleasant things
- Is sympathetic

If your employee is a JUDGING type, it is likely that he or she:

- Likes to have things decided and settled
- Is more decisive than curious
- Lives according to plans
- Lives according to standards and customs not easily or lightly set aside
- Tries to make situations conform to own standards
- Makes definite choices from among the possibilities
- Is uneasy with unplanned happenings
- Bases friendships upon shared beliefs, standards, and tastes
- Has enduring friendships
- Sets up "shoulds" and "oughts" and judges self against them
- Aims to be right
- Is self-regimented, purposeful, and exacting
- Is orderly, organized, and systematic
- Likes assignments to be clear and definite
- Has settled opinions
- May be tolerant of routine procedure

If your employee is a PERCEPTIVE type, it is likely that he or she:

- Is more curious than decisive
- Lives according to the situation of the movement
- May not plan things but act spontaneously
- Is comfortable in handling the unplanned
- Looks for new experiences & expects to be interested
- Samples many more experiences than can be digested or used
- Takes a "live and let live" attitude
- Bases friendships on propinquity and shared experiences
- Takes on friendships easily
- Aims to miss nothing
- Is flexible, adaptable, and tolerant
- Wants to understand things more than manage them
- Leaves things open
- Has trouble making decisions
- Starts too many projects & has difficulty finishing them
- Postpones unpleasant jobs
- Welcomes new light on a thing or situation

Source: Lawrence (1982), pp. 69-77.

sion-oriented. Eighty-two percent of the outer-directed were Sensing; 52 percent of the inner-directed were Intuitive. Thus it is
possible to infer whether a group is apt to be inner-directed or
outer-directed by observation along the dimensions of Table 8.2.

So what? To what end have I introduced the MBTI? Where are
we going? Simply put, in order to put a potentially successful segmentation scheme into place, one needs to determine what communications strategies to use to reach each of those segments selected
as targets, because if the groups are divided meaningfully, the
method of communication successfully used with one group may
fail abysmally when used for another.

Most of my work, both as a consultant and as a teacher, has been
where "the rubber meets the road"–implementing the strategic
insights that someone has had (sometimes me, either alone or as part
of a team). The best strategy in the world or the best and most
accurate segmentation scheme will avail nothing if the implementation of the strategy or segmentation scheme is inept. There is a large
amount of literature devoted to the end of strategic planning (Stacey,
1992, cited earlier is an example); I think much of the criticism of
planning is not truly criticism of the concept of planning so much as
of the implementation (or lack of implementation) of plans by organizations in the past.

One scholar who has devoted extensive attention to implementing
marketing strategy is Thomas Bonoma of Harvard University. In the
Preface to his MBA-level textbook, he states ". . . I sometimes tell
my students that what I teach is driver's education. As we remember, there is a theory of parallel parking . . . but getting the car
perfectly wedged between a Lamborghini and a Mack truck is a
different matter entirely" (Bonoma, 1984b:ix). I like the metaphor;
the theory of driving a car does need to be known and mastered
before one can be considered a good driver; nevertheless, simply
mastering the theory (or using a computer simulator) does not guar-
antee mastery once one turns the key in a real car.

Bonoma focuses on bridging gaps between the system and the
individual, claiming that it is possible to substitute personal skills
for weak structures. After studying numerous marketing organizations, he found that in the best companies, a strong sense of identity
and direction in marketing policies; these firms continually appealed

to customers in unusual ways (the Marketing Concept again, although he never calls it that). Management can and does substitute skill for system, and top management understands the importance of implementation to the firm's success (Bonoma, 1984a). (See Figure 8.2 for a representation of implementation/problem diagnosis.) Bonoma calls the substitution of skills for systems "subversion" (1986); as such, it fits within much of the recent practitioner writing imploring people to "steal time" to develop new products, to manage by throwing away the policy manuals, etc. Cross, Belick, and Rudelius (1990) report on a survey on how marketing managers use segmentation. The results of the survey? They use the results variously. No big surprise here!

FIGURE 8.2. Marketing Strategy and Implementation Problem Diagnosis

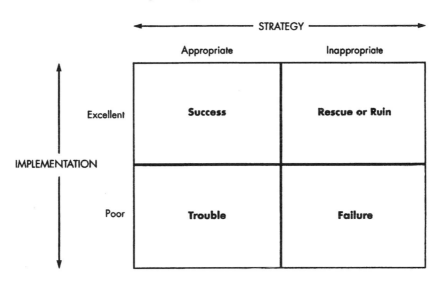

Source: Adapted from Bonoma (1981), p. 72.

Chapter 9

Finally:
Which Segmentation Technique?

Which segmentation technique do we use? Psychographics? Expensive, whether one subscribes to a syndicated service or does it oneself. Demographics? Crude and unsophisticated—and probably not very good. The tried-and-true segment of marketing folklore—women aged eighteen to forty-nine—may describe the buyer of many products, particularly household consumer products bought in grocery and drug stores, but can no longer describe the users—and we know we need to segment for the users, not just the buyer—and probably no longer describes as many buyers as it used to, with more men shopping (either because they are heads of households or simply doing the shopping) and more teenagers doing the family's weekly shopping.

Can we objectively evaluate which segmentation strategy to use? Segmentation claims that it helps marketers by giving them direction in designing advertisements that appeal to and reach specifically segmented groups. Can we test for this? Certainly; direct marketing does this sort of thing all the time.

Christen (1987) reports on "richness curves"—a technique which shows how much better the marketer can do by segmenting the market than by simply using a base rate (no segmentation) in targeting those customers who are more likely to buy the product or service (the richer segments). This, of course, is exactly what Hallberg (1995) has implored marketers to do; this is what direct marketing tries to do. Christen's research was based on using three demographic variables (household income, age, and education) versus household income alone; no surprise—the three variables did a better job. He states, however, "I suspect that psychographic segmentation would look much more useful when evaluated through an appropriate index such as richness" (1987:20) rather than R or R^2 as it usually is. Richness was one of the criteria that was used to help design the segments for VALS 2 (Novak, de Leeuw, and MacEvoy, 1992).

I would like to return to something that Bonoma and Shapiro (1983) and Shapiro and Bonoma (1983) discuss in their nested segmentation strategy for industrial markets. Their point is to segment only as deeply in the nest as necessary. This is a good lesson for any segmentation scheme. If demographic segmentation gets the job done for you, fine; it may be difficult to hold your head up in the country club locker room if your firm is only targeting that mythical "eighteen to forty-nine woman," but your shareholders will like the fact that you are not spending much on segmentation schemes and still selling goods and services. If, however, straight demographics is no longer working, than geodemographics may be necessary. And so on.

This may strike some readers as heresy, particularly the ones who know me and my past commitment to VALS and my ongoing love of psychographics, perceptual mapping, understanding the customer in depth as required by the Marketing Concept, etc. However, the cost of understanding the customer in depth has to be acknowledged and the use of marketing resources to do so questioned constantly. The use of psychographics to build a complex segmentation model for a small chain of hotels whose basic appeal is "low price/no frills/small rooms" is questionable. Particularly if the group which typically patronizes the motel keeps the occupancy rate in the 90 percent range. Psychographics may be nice to know, it might be icing on the cake, but if it does not increase customer satisfaction, if it does not increase sales, if it does not increase profitability, than it is information that fails to deliver any result.

The engineering maxim of "KISS"–"keep it simple, stupid"– applies to segmentation as to so many other areas of marketing. We may applaud sophistication, we may relish an elegant solution. But we pay for answers, and the simpler the answer, usually, the smaller the bill.

APPENDIX:
CASE APPLICATIONS
OF SEGMENTATION

Introduction to the Cases

Some of the power of using a segmentation strategy can be seen in the following case studies. The first study involves using VALS as a language to enable everyone in a widely dispersed and quite diverse corporation to discuss their customers with a common vocabulary; the second study involves the use of VALS to segment focus group respondents and get a feel for the way people in each major segment in the firm's target market describe houses in an attempt to redesign several different products and services; the third is a description of developing and using a proprietary segmentation scheme.

One of the reasons for the material covered in Part III is the belief that I hold, driven home by fifteen years of reading, research, and practice, that strategy must be translated into practice—but it must be translated through research. There is no substitute for directed research into a firm's market, customers, employees, and product(s). Without such research, a firm is flying completely blind. With a directed, programmatic approach to strategy implementation through research, the important questions may come up in a meaningful sequence and be answered in a meaningful sequence.

CASE 1: VALSPEAK
AND AN ORGANIZATION'S CULTURE

Organizational culture is a problematic concept. There are probably as many definitions of organizational culture as there are academic authors who attempt to tackle the subject. Schein (1985) defines it as a "pattern of basic assumptions" of a given group. Kilmann, Saxton, and Serpa (1986) define it as the "shared philosophies, ideologies, values, assumptions, beliefs, expectations, attitudes, and norms that knit a community together." Smircich (1983) reviews the concepts and definitions primarily in the organizational literature. Ouchi and Wilkins (1985) review the literature with a historical perspective, noting the shift of authors from faculty in sociology and anthropology departments to those disciplines which reside in management departments. Deshpande and Webster (1989) attempt to move the definitions and concept of organizational culture over to marketing where its importance is "undeniable."

Despite this academic difficulty in defining the term, managers seem intuitively to know exactly what "organizational culture" is and why it is important. Some of this knowledge undoubtedly is derived from *In Search of Excellence* (Peters and Waterman, 1982) and the ensuing books, articles, television programs, and news segments on "strong cultures" and their importance to American industry and competitiveness. (For a counter to some of this outpouring, see Saffold [1988].) What follows is a description of one company's organizational culture and the effects on that culture of a major change imposed by management.

DECOY was founded in the late 1950s to publish and print weekly newspapers. Always a technological leader, DECOY was among the first printers outside the New York City area to use web-offset and cold type. In the 1960s DECOY entered the real estate publishing market with *Homes Illustrated*, magazines which depict houses for sale with both text and photographs and were distributed free to prospective homebuyers. By the late 1980s, DECOY was publishing approximately twenty weekly suburban newspapers, twenty *Homes Illustrated* magazines, and one weekly real estate newspaper, covering cities from southern California to northern Ohio.

DECOY has continued in the technological forefront, and was among the first to use laser cameras and digital typesetting equipment. In 1977, DECOY began the development of *CompuAd*, a computer program which writes classified advertisements for houses. By the late 1980s, several hundred copies of *CompuAd* and its progeny had been sold in the United States and overseas.

The main reason for DECOY's success is, without a doubt, the Chairman and founder. The holder of degrees from two Ivy League colleges, he put together a successful company through a combination of hard work, vision, and top people who were both good at what they did and also complementary to the skills of the Chairman. By his own admission not much of an administrator, he also has an extremely low threshold of boredom. Therefore, his senior people need to have the ability to pick up his intellectual "dirty clothes" where he has dropped them and carry projects through to their conclusion. He has consistently been able to find such people.

The corporate culture of DECOY in 1986 could only be described as open. The Chairman and other managers were readily accessible to everyone in the company. Further, there was little structure and almost no written job descriptions among senior managers. The concept of "corporate staff" did not exist, so almost anyone could be assigned to any special project–matrix management by default. The individual newspaper and magazine operations were highly autonomous, with almost no formal reporting requirements from the manager to the Chairman. Except for financial data, the only reporting consisted of telephone conversations, usually initiated by the Chairman when he wished to know "what's going on." Failure was rarely punished by termination; after thirty years in business, the Chairman was proud to announce that he had fired only two people. Displeasure was, rather, evidenced by a noticeable coolness in relations with the Chairman. People were intensely loyal to the Chairman; when a program of awarding service pins was initiated in 1989, several twenty-five-year pins were given to relatively low-level employees.

A striking feature of the firm's culture was the fact that none of the entities identified itself as "A DECOY Company" until many months or even years after the introduction of that name. All the entities were known by their own names and most of their local advertisers–and most of the advertisers for all the entities were local–though the publications were locally owned. The DECOY name was introduced, appeared on the mastheads of some of the publications, and no general explanation of what DECOY was or why the name was being changed was made to either advertisers or employees. In early 1989, DECOY started a newsletter to its almost 500 employees to present DECOY and its entities to itself; it was with great reluctance that the Chairman was persuaded to write a couple of articles about who DECOY was and why it mattered. He felt that these facts should have been self-evident to his employees.

But the most noticeable feature of DECOY's culture was the firm's drive to innovate, both in improvements to current products and in the creation of new products. DECOY's innovation is directly attributable to the Chairman. Blessed with an inquiring mind, he continually asked questions beginning with "Why can't we?" or "Why doesn't?"–questions that often led to innovative solutions to problems. Because he let his managers manage, he had no difficulty "taking time from the same old grind" (Berton, 1989) for innovation. In fact, innovation frequently took precedence over operations, often to the distress of the managers.

DECOY embodied several of Pearson's (1988) five key activities which make some firms innovators, despite not having a clear structure or strategic focus. These activities are:

1. Creating an environment that values performance above all else
2. Structuring to permit innovative ideas to rise above the demands of operations–or in this case, having no real structure
3. Defining a focus that lets the company channel its innovation realistically
4. Knowing where to look for good ideas
5. Going after good ideas full speed

A danger of having the Chairman lead the innovation effort is that it becomes difficult to stop a bad idea, particularly when it is the Chairman's own. Staw (1976), Ross and Staw (1993) and Staw and Ross (1987a, 1987b) have written extensively on escalation of commitment and its causes; DECOY had continual difficulty in killing off projects that had become marginal (Hisrich and Cahill, 1995). This problem is possibly caused by the fact that the source of so much innovation at DECOY is the Chairman. According to DECOY folklore, *CompuAd* started one day when the Chairman, reacting to the stream of bad advertising copy received by *Homes Illustrated* from real estate agents, asked "Can't we get a computer to write this stuff better?" After an investment of several years and hundreds of thousands of dollars, the answer is unequivocally "yes."

Since DECOY was in two quite different industries–newspapers and real estate publishing–there was no common language across the industries. Their only commonality was that both products were printed on newsprint. In one division the customers were almost exclusively real estate firms and their agents; in the other, customers were mostly retailers and individual subscribers. Both newspaper managers and *Homes Illustrated* managers had a good feel for what their advertisers wanted and needed, but used different terminology to articulate that feel to corporate staff. Communication as a cultural performance (Pacanowsky and O'Donnell-Trujillo 1983) was difficult to decipher in these circumstances as there were multiple subcultures (if not true multiple cultures) within the firm. Thus, the corporate office wound up with a confused sense of who DECOY's customers were. This was not auspicious for continued long-term success as the 1980s drew to a close (M. Miller, 1987).

DECOY's Chairman had first heard of VALS through an *Atlantic* magazine article (Atlas, 1984). His curiosity was aroused by VALS's purported ability to explain how "two people living next door to each other with the same basic demographic profile live so differently and buy such different things." Despite the presence of literally dozens of other typologies, VALS is well known by the business public and is relatively easy to explain to those who do not know it. These facts make it attractive to managers dealing with business-to-business marketing problems, and advertisers intent on improving their communications with their clients' customers (Maher, 1983). After attending the VALS users' conference in November, 1987, and finding himself in congenial company—an important consideration in many small, family-run firms and especially true in DECOY—the Chairman committed DECOY to using VALS in the marketing of both *CompuAd* and *Homes Illustrated*.

The strategy for *CompuAd* was to use VALS to write more powerful and targeted advertisements. The computer could be programmed to create different advertisements for the same house to appeal to different VALS types. This ability would lead to more inquiries per ad, thus making *CompuAd* more valuable to its users. *Homes Illustrated* was to be redesigned to accommodate ads written for the different VALS types. DECOY hoped that SRI's experience in real estate gained with their work with Ray Ellison Builders of San Antonio would help DECOY better focus its products and produce better advertising and promotional materials for the products. DECOY's primary corporate goal for using VAL3 was to have all its personnel speaking the same language about the firm's customers. James Tilton, then Vice President at Ray Ellison Builders, claimed that the "greatest value of VALS is in sensitizing Ellison to the customers and *their* values" (Tilton 1988)—not a goal to belittle in this day of better customer service and concern about "quality".

As part of the VALS subscription, DECOY elected to have SRI come to Cleveland in February, 1988, to deliver an orientation to most of the management of the corporation as well as the managers of the newspaper division. The VALS orientation included a slide show, videotapes, and role-playing exercises to familiarize individuals with the VALS types. At the end of the day-long session, most of the attendees had a rudimentary understanding of VALS and what the individuals of the various types were like.

DECOY's corporate staff was then charged with the task of developing an in-depth understanding of VALS to connect it to the various projects under way at DECOY. By far the most important task was to disseminate the VALS language about customers and the population at large among DECOY's employees. All managers were given extreme latitude in running their operations: headquarters help was available if needed, but so long as the operation was profitable, supervision was minimal. Cross-communication, even within the same "division" was infrequent; managers usually communicated with headquarters which then disseminated information to the various operations. Attempting to impose change on this most loosely coupled of systems imaginable was not going to be easy.

And yet, there was immense change. DECOY's culture allowed for—in fact, almost demanded—easy introduction of innovations. The Chairman's dictum that DECOY would adopt VALS throughout the firm gave corporate staff the foot in the door with anyone who might be recalcitrant. Within a short time of the orientation meeting, all of DECOY's people were talking about "Belongers" and "Achievers" and "Soc Cons" ("Societally Conscious") as though these terms had been part of the DECOY lexicon forever. DECOY *had* successfully adopted VALS as a corporate-wide language. Given a sufficient amount of time and effort, it should have been possible to make the sophisticated use of the typology second nature to key employees at most of the entities. The managers had, without realizing it, been crying out for such a communications tool for a long time. These managers were a willing body of disciples for adoption.

However, to the disappointment of both corporate staff and the Chairman, the ancillary uses of VALS came to naught at DECOY. There were only two rather feeble attempts to VALS-type markets for DECOY products. A haphazardly chosen sample of *CompuAd* users was VALS typed with marginal results and no follow-through. Readers of one DECOY newspaper who requested information were sent a VALS-typing questionnaire to be returned. There was no follow-through with these returned questionnaires. Markets were to be VALS typed prior to the introduction of two new products as a now-standard part of the new product research and development process. When the new product introductions were stopped, so was the VALS typing. An abortive attempt to do a "quick-and-dirty" VALS typing at an interactive computer terminal for a new product was stopped before the algorithms were sketched.

Several attempts were made to tie VALS directly into one of the newspapers and the *CompuAd/NewsAd* family of real estate software—primarily through the use of words, symbols, or design elements which would appeal to one or more of the types. A prototype of a future *NewsAd* could write two advertisements for the same house for different VALS types—one for Achievers and one for the Societally Conscious—with a single input of data, thus proving that the concept was sound. An advertisement for *NewsAd 2* was directed squarely at Achievers. When a major new marketing effort was launched in 1989 for *NewsAd 2,* there was a pair of media advertisements produced, one aimed at Achievers and the other at the Societally Conscious. These were the most promising developments of VALS "technology" to the DECOY product line.

Was DECOY's VALS attempt worth the effort? The unifying factor of a common language provided a large enough benefit by itself to make the effort not only worthwhile, but a success. DECOY did not make any more marketing use of its adoption of VALS than it did of its own name change. Most DECOY customers did not know that the firm was a VALS subscriber, nor were they advised how to use VALS in *their* marketing efforts. VALS was never adequately used to gain a competitive edge for DECOY. One reason for this fact was the introduction of VALS 2 so soon after DECOY subscribed to VALS. A second reason was also the culture at DECOY, where operational decisions were left to the entities and not dictated by headquarters. When the entities raised potential uses for VALS, the Chairman never stated that he espoused such use. Despite all the shortcomings in the implementation of VALS, in SRI's handling of its product, and in VALS itself, the effort at least operated at "breakeven" and probably was a net benefit to this highly fragmented firm.

CASE 2: TYPING FOCUS GROUPS FOR PRODUCT/SERVICE DESIGN

During the spring of 1988, DECOY Inc., commissioned National Market Measures to hold a series of focus group sessions to determine if people classified into groups based on differing psychographic profiles (in this case, VALS types) reacted in ways sufficiently different from each other to suggest that segmented marketing, beginning at the product design level, would lead to greater marketing returns (National Market Measures, 1988). Three goals were the focus of the research:

1. To see if the different groups responded differently to different house styles
2. To see if the different groups demanded different information beyond the photograph of the house in classified advertisements
3. To see if the different groups responded differently to the choice of different words and symbols in classified advertisements

National Market Measures (NMM) was commissioned to hold three focus groups: one each for Belongers, Achievers, and the Societally Conscious—the three VALS types which DECOY hypothesized had the greatest importance for real estate publishing because of the size of the groups and their income and wealth levels. Nationally, Belongers constituted 38 percent of the population, Achievers, 20 percent; and the Societally Conscious were 12 percent (Ploss, 1987). In the Cleveland area, Belongers were 35 percent, Achievers, 31 percent; and the Societally Conscious 12 percent (WJW-TV8,

1988). Thus, with three focus groups, DECOY could have data from the three VALS types which represented over two-thirds of the adult population, and a considerably larger percentage of the house-buying population. It was hoped that the information which came out of the research would be usable in the geographically dispersed markets served by DECOY (Lesser and Hughes, 1986); in fact, this national scope of the segments was one of the attractions of VALS.

NMM used telephone solicitation with a screening questionnaire which disguised the subject to be covered, but did ascertain that the respondent was either "actively in the market to buy a house or had recently bought or sold a house." Those respondents who agreed to participate were sent the VALS questionnaire and typed; only those who were Belongers, Achievers, or Societally Conscious were to be recontacted and scheduled for a group. However, one problem surfaced during the VALS typing: there were insufficient Societally Conscious individuals who were "actively" in the market to form a group. The decision was made to include enough Experientials (5 percent of the national market and 6.5 percent in Cleveland) to have a full group of "Inner-Directeds," as this "track" was deemed important enough to warrant a separate focus group.

Once the focus group participants were at NMM's facilities, they were shown color photographs of ten houses, all of which were approximately $3'' \times 5''$, and which were arrayed on two flip charts in roughly the chronological order in which the house styles appeared. These houses were all actually for sale (although none were in Cleveland) and were deliberately chosen to represent house styles that were commonly found in Cleveland. Although they were cut out of several different for-sale magazines and represented several different real estate markets, they were all listed in the $300,000 to $500,000 range; the participants were told that price of the house would not matter, that they were to assume that they could afford any of the houses that they would be shown. At this point, there were only three questions which DECOY really wanted answered:

1. Which houses(s) did each VALS type prefer?
2. What further information would each VALS type (and all the respondents, regardless of VALS type) wish to see in an ad for that house?

3. What language did each VALS type use to talk about the houses?

The focus groups were conducted at a facility designed for such groups by a trained moderator under the usual circumstances in May and August 1988. The Achiever group that was held in May was problematical, as previously mentioned. Thus, ultimately, there were four groups: Belongers with six participants; Inner-Directed with nine participants; Achiever #1 with nine; and Achiever #2 with ten participants.

With regard to Question 1–did the groups respond differently to the different house styles presented–the answer is clearly "Yes." Although there is some overlap among the groups–"Tudor Revival" being picked by both the Inner-Directed and Achievers, and "Modern" and "Norman/French Revival" being picked by both Achievers and Belongers, the rank order was different except for Modern, and the reasons given by participants for the choices were quite different. These reasons will be discussed later.

With regard to Question 2–what information was needed beyond the photograph–there were similarities among the VALS types as well as differences. All participants regardless of VALS type stressed the need for location, price, size of house and/or size of lot–the "usual" stuff. The Inner Directed wanted some indication of the interesting features and overall *gestalt* of the house. They were willing to overlook the absence of a list of features in return for more psychological attributes, mostly in the nature of making the house more "interesting"–a key word for this group. The Achievers wanted to know about utilities, how long the house had been on the market, and the age of the house. But their biggest need was that the house appear to be a trophy, a visible sign of the fact that they have "made it." The Belongers had a very narrow list of information requirements: size of the kitchen, size and number of closets and bedrooms, as well as what school district the house was in. Overall, however, the Belongers seemed to express the need for location being the primary criterion for their choice. All of the information desired by all groups can, of course, be obtained by a tour of the house and grounds; the above data is what these VALS types want in order to make the decision to make the tour and is thus crucial to include in advertisements designed to make them want to come look.

Question 3–the different word choices and symbols to use in classified advertisements for the different VALS types–remains unanswered by this research. So much time was spent in determining favored house style and lists of features that the groups spent insufficient time developing the word lists. One would like to work with this word list in conjunction with McCracken's concept of "Diderot Unities" mentioned earlier to see if this concept holds for *verbalization* about goods as well as the goods themselves. The groups provided insufficient data but there are indications here of what might be apparent "hot buttons" to reach different VALS types in advertisements.

There are really two different sets of implications of this research: implications for DECOY and others in their real estate publication efforts, and wider implications for real estate brokerage firms and real estate development firms. To take the second implication first, it is clear that the different VALS types view house styles differently. Although only the Inner Directed group seemed comfortable putting "correct" names on the different house styles, different styles clearly appealed to different groups and, at least as important, three styles–"Contemporary," "NeoVictorian," and "Colonial"–were no one's favorite and few participants could find a kind word to say about any of these three. It would be beneficial for a developer to be careful in choosing which house styles to put in a development, unless it was the developer's conscious choice to try to mix the three VALS types studied here.

It was the answer to Question 2–what information beyond the picture would be needed by each group–that holds the greatest interest. One of the participants stated that he needed "nothing–the picture says it all." This statement, although more extreme than the other participants were willing to go, was basically confirmed by the rest of the Achievers around the table. The sentiment was confirmed by the auditors at SRI as being quite consistent with one of the differences between Achievers and the Inner Directed: the Inner Directed like to read lots of copy in an advertisement, while Achievers will not read much.

It should then be theoretically possible to design a single publication to reach both Achievers and the Inner Directed with advertisements that only the targeted group would "see," even though there were two ads for a single house. The Inner Directed ad would have a small picture and lots of copy; the Achiever ad would have an enormous picture and a headline containing only the information mentioned above as vital to Achievers. In fact, after listening to the groups, it became apparent that the Inner Directed had the uncanny ability to look "through" the pictures presented to them and categorically state what the inside layout of the house was, down to floor plans and window locations on the sides away from the camera.

It is clear, even from the exceedingly preliminary nature of this research, that there are differences in how houses are perceived by different people—even when the houses are viewed only in $3'' \times 5''$ color photographs. Using a psychographic typology such as VALS to segment respondents sharpens differences between houses. Jack Nasar, using an intercept study where his researchers showed people stylized drawings of six house types to determine which house people would feel most comfortable about approaching if they needed help; in which house would someone who was a "Take charge" individual live; and which house would people choose if they won a "dream house" lottery. Nasar found that there were clear differences between house types on these dimensions, although there is no indication that he tried to differentiate between types of people in his sample (Freudenheim, 1988; Nasar, 1988a, 1989). Sadalla, Vershure, and Burroughs (1987) performed different research with similar results—that our houses reflect who we are. Shortly after his research was published, Nasar started using images of real buildings captured on a TrueVision graphics computer system "manipulated for appropriate control," because he felt that the drawings he had previously used might produce ambiguous results (Nasar, 1988b). The need to control landscape features in this fashion was pointed up by all three VALS types commenting upon the "Contemporary" house's lack of established trees—even though it apparently overlooks a forested valley.

It is evident that, unless house styles are intermingled in a neighborhood, the likelihood of different VALS types of the same income level living in that neighborhood is lowered. The Inner Directed would not be comfortable in Achiever houses, and vice versa. The above has great potential meaning in at least two respects. First is the fact that mixing house styles is uncommon in new housing developments; therefore, the likelihood of different VALS types living together is at least hypothetically higher in older, more "organic" communities. Second is the fact that it is at least theoretically possible for lifestyle or psychographic data to be used by other than marketers—planners for example—in an attempt to plan the future growth and trends for their cities. As an example of this latter application, two suburbs of Cleveland—Cleveland Heights and Lakewood—seem remarkably similar demographically. They are both older (early 1900s), first-ring suburbs whose housing stock and population demographics are similar. Anyone familiar with Cleveland, however, would recognize that there is "something" different between the two communities; it is unlikely that someone living in Lakewood would feel comfortable in Cleveland Heights or vice versa. A psychographic or lifestyle portrait of the two communities should discover what that "something" is in a fashion that would enable the planner to understand the community better.

However, it is also clear from this project that there are distinct and meaningful differences among individuals in the real estate market which the VALS typology is identifying. The responses of the Inner Directed participants resembled each other far more than they did the Achiever participants.

CASE 3: A PROPRIETARY SEGMENTATION SCHEME

DECOY, Inc., as mentioned previously, did not renew its subscription to VALS 2 after a one-year trial. There were many frustrations with SRI and its development of VALS 2, but these could have been easily overcome. What could not be overcome, however, was the lack of a research stream for VALS 2 such as had been built up over the years for VALS. As previously mentioned, this is one of the advantages to buying a syndicated rather than proprietary segmentation scheme. In late 1990, DECOY contracted with American LIVES to create a segmentation scheme dealing only with homeowners/buyers and the types of houses they lived in and desired.

In March and April of 1991, American LIVES conducted a random sample survey of the Denver real estate market (American LIVES, 1991). The survey sampled Denver housing sales for the previous eighteen months. Of 1,153 valid names and address of recent home buyers acquired from a mailing list service to whom surveys were mailed, there was a return of approximately 500 questionnaires, for a 43 percent response rate. American LIVES deemed the response rate adequate for all the statistical analyses to be performed for the segmentation study.

The survey asked questions never before systematically examined in a real estate market (although some were previously asked in DECOY research—see National Market Measures, 1985). The questionnaire was jointly developed by DECOY personnel and American LIVES personnel. The instrument was eleven pages long (much too long, in my experience—the return rate is astronomical in the face of this fact) and explored many unclear items, which American LIVES hoped would lead to shorter questionnaires in future studies. The survey is unique in that it covered the home search process (see Cahill, 1994c for the results of this aspect), desire for house features and the use of the house by the different segments, house style analysis, and values and demographics (the LIVES analysis proper— Lifestyle, Interests, Values, Expectations, and Symbols of the house buyer).

The questionnaire was designed with several kinds of questions, which taken together give a rich basis for the analysis and segmentation:

- Why they moved
- The house search process
- Type, size, and price of house
- How they sold their previous house
- Preference for preowned or new house
- Intentions for the next time they sell a house
- Attitudes toward realtors and their quality of service
- Information and services used in house search
- Preferences for neighborhood and area feature
- Preferences for exterior house features
- Preferences for interior house features

- Different uses for rooms
- Values and lifestyles
- Demographics

American LIVES then did a LIVES segmentation on the data derived that was tied specifically to Denver and yet could also satisfy Decoy's strategic needs for the *Homes* magazine markets. The primary applications of a LIVES segmentation are in a wide variety of businesses whose products are complex or expensive, symbolically loaded, a key part of someone's lifestyle, reflective of what is most meaningful in consumers' lives and sold differently to different groups. Examples of products or services this approach works well for include cars, consumer electronics, and vacation travel. Houses all but define the array.

The LIVES segmentation model follows two principles (American LIVES, 1991): first, all people organize their lives around their values and lifestyles. Different groups in the population employ very different values and lifestyles; the use of the values and lifestyle measures gives very stable market segments that are based on what anthropologists and sociologists call subcultures. Second, consumers try to make their lives more meaningful and consistent in terms of a few basic ideas. The segmentation scheme does not have to come up with a large list of descriptors of peoples' way of life, for some ideas are more basic than others. If this sounds somewhat like the VALS segmentation principles, perhaps it is because one of the developers of the LIVES scheme worked for VALS while Arnold Mitchell was still alive. Perhaps that helps explain why it all seems to make sense.

The returned questionnaires were analyzed along the underlying dimensions of what is most important in the lives of the home buyers; five subcultures, which were christened "Tribes" for ease of communication, were discovered: Winners, Authenticks, Wannabes, Heartlanders, and Maintainers.

Winners, representing 23 percent of the market, were the most upscale group in the survey. Seventy-six percent were managers and professionals, 68 percent had incomes over $50,000 (versus 38 percent of the sample), while 21 percent had incomes over $100,000. The median income was $55,000 (versus $38,000 for the sample), and 50 percent had attended or completed graduate school. The median age was thirty-eight years, the same as the sample. In terms of values, this group was extremely status- and success-oriented; they were business conservatives and relatively family-oriented. The median price of their house was $98,000, *versus* the sample's $85,000; 44 percent bought a house priced over $120,000 (versus the sample's 20 percent). This group dominated the high-priced house market, both new houses and resales. They liked all the status features in a house and liked to have a luxury look in some rooms. They wanted a "Big House," a trophy house, in a mature, status neighborhood. The male/female split was 60 percent/40 percent.

Winners are the most visible buyers in the real estate market. Realtors and home builders are most familiar with them because they identify most with them. Winners focus their attention on self, work, and family, in that order. They are knowledgeable and savvy house buyers who know what they want and want to buy it efficiently. They are materialistic to a fault, and technologically aware. The house should reflect their sense of themselves: stylish and good-looking. They want to see a lot of variation in styles and front elevations and want a lot of choices in what they buy.

Authenticks, representing 18 percent of the market, were the secondmost upscale group. Fifty-three percent were managers and professionals, and 45 percent percent have incomes over $50,000; the median family income was $41,000. Twenty-seven percent attended or completed graduate school. This group is evenly split between male and female. The median house price was $85,000; this group is dominant in the preowned-house-in-established-neighborhoods market. Their house is expected to be a nest, hidden away from the world, with no big statement to the street, nor any status or luxury features inside or out, but with a big, well-equipped kitchen. They want to be close to nature.

Authenticks are individualists, for all their broad social concerns, so their tastes are more personalized than those of other groups. They care more about being unique than they do in owning what is unique. They are well-educated, creative, and self-confident. They are psychologically sophisticated with a low tolerance for being "sold to"; many hate builders and realtors and feel that they are dumb, have poor taste, and the wrong values to deal with the

Authenticks. Their house is a way to show their creativity, so they want a preowned house that they can invest with their own personal touch and their own meanings and values. Family is less important to them and it often shows in their house choices. These are the natural leaders for innovation in many consumer goods, so innovative houses also appeal. Their values in general are also nontraditional.

Heartlanders, representing 21 percent of the market, were the oldest group, with a median age of forty-one years; almost a third were over fifty–and partly because of their age, they dominated the empty-nester market. Their income was about average; median income was $35,000. Their education was slightly below average– high school graduates with some college. The male/female split was 35percent/65 percent. The median price of their house was at the sample median, but Heartlanders had more equity in the house because of their age. They wanted to be in built-up, very accessible parts of the city–but in very secure neighborhoods. A "plain vanilla" house would do–simple, comfortable, practical, with no status features. Their notion of a house is extremely conventional and conformist; they will reject all the innovative features which attract the Authenticks.

Heartlanders are the antithesis of the Authenticks; they are conformists who lack broad social concerns, with very little personalization of taste. They are traditionalists who do not feel comfortable in the modern world, who want their path through life to be narrow, well-lit, and well posted. They long for a nostalgic, idealized image of the way things were in small towns around the turn of the century. The religious right is strongest in this group; they are very intolerant of both Winners' emphasis on what they see as greed, materialism, and status display as well as the Authenticks' "way-outness." They want to surround themselves with clear and well-marked boundaries that show symbolically that they live in a safe haven. Safety and security are far more important than status display or innovation.

Wannabes, representing 23 percent of the market, were the youngest group with a median age of thirty-six; 29 percent are under thirty. Their median income was $31,000; they had below average education–high school and some college–in part reflective of their youth. Their occupations were mostly sales, services, and technical support. The male/female split was 41 percent/59 percent. The median price of their house was $72,000, the lowest of any group; most have grudgingly had to settle for less of a house than they wanted, They wanted to have locations close to shopping and work. They lusted for nearly all house features, especially status and luxury; they wanted all features more than any other group. They expected to overextend themselves financially on a purchase. They felt their house should be loaded with features, even if it had to be small and below average in price; a nest, hidden away from the world; but with a front elevation that makes a big statement to the world—even if the front is just a facade.

Wannabes are imitators of Winners and define their lifestyles, values, and house preferences in what they perceive the Winners to have, want, and be. Actually, however, they do not have a clear vision of what the Winners are, have, do, or want. Instead, they tend to operate from a stereotypical set of attitudes formed from a distance, so the features they desire are exaggerated. Their vision of the "good life" is what Winners have—period. They are obsessed with success and status, but have not cracked the code for success and status. They are young and ambitious, but their lack of education will tend to work against them. Ongoing income constraints will prevent them from getting very much of what they want; thus, they help define the bottom of the preowned house market. Their champagne tastes, which are longings rather than experiences, confront the dismal fact of their current—and probably future—beer budgets. They simply lack the education and job skills to move up.

Maintainers, representing 16 percent of the market, were the most downscale group, with many blue-collar workers. They and the Wannabes had the lowest median income at $31,000; but Maintainers had the lowest education in the sample, with high school (and some college, but less than the Wannabes). Their median age was thirty-nine, with a male/female split of 53 percent/47 percent. Their median house price was $76,000, well below the sample. They wanted fewer features than the other groups and wanted them less strongly. What they appear to want is the small, cheap, plain, fixer-upper house—basic shelter. They were the group most likely to try to buy a "For Sale by Owner," to save on the realtor's commission. They, like the Wannabes, wanted locations that were close to shopping and to work. In many respects, Maintainers are simply Wannabes who have aged and know that they have lost the possibility of succeeding.

Maintainers are often the people who fix your car or television set. Life has passed them by and they know it; they are very cynical, alienated, and discouraged about values. The few positive responses Maintainers make to values are patriotism, macho attitudes, and sports. Men are less interested in family life. Physical activities such as sports, hunting, fishing, tinkering with cars or the house are likely to define their leisure lives, as well as watching television. It appears that they see the values espoused by other groups as a sham and are unalterably opposed to the values espoused by the Authenticks. They define the bottom of the preowned house market. They are also the least likely to see realtors or read a homes magazine—or, in fact, to read much of anything.

DECOY, Inc., immediately took this new segmentation scheme to heart, much as they had taken the VALS scheme to heart, as outlined in Case 1. Within a few months of the study in Denver, a presentation had been developed and shown to customers around the country; further, the *CompuAd* family of software was refined to take the new scheme into account when writing its advertisements. When the scheme, truly applicable only to Denver, was shown to realtors elsewhere, they all nodded in agreement and said that it matched their experiences with customers in their markets. It is so VALS-like that it carries the same surface validity with it. DECOY has been happy with their results and has not felt impelled to replicate the study elsewhere, nor to bring the study up to date—the results are now five years old.

WHAT DO THE CASES TELL US?

These are three cases of different implementation of segmentation schemes. I could go on for other examples, in different industries or with different sized firms, but I think my point is made. Implementation is the step which separates the successful firms from the less-successful firms. The scheme does not need to be sophisticated, simply successfully implemented. A real estate firm in northern Ohio has carved out a niche of customers which it feels to be important—first time buyers—and is lavishing advertising and other marketing attention upon this niche. These people are not easy to find; there is no medium which caters to the first-time house buyer. Much of this firm's advertising expenditure necessarily spills over to second-, third-, forth-time buyers; however, much of the message is directed solely at the first-time buyers, and they are responding to the message quite well—successful implementation of a rather crude segmenting scheme. It is possible. It is not easy. But, if accomplished, it is profitable, and that *is* the goal, isn't it?

References

Alsop, Ronald (1987). "Agencies Scrutinize Their Ads for Psychological Symbolism." *The Wall Street Journal* (June 11), p. 25.

American LIVES (1991). Study of the Denver Real Estate Market. San Francisco.

Anderson, W. Thomas, Jr., Linda L. Golden, U. N. Umesh, and William A. Weeks (1989). "The Five Faces of Eve: Women's Timestyle Typologies," in Thomas K. Srull (ed.). *Advances in Consumer Research*, Vol. 16. Provo, UT: Association for Consumer Research, pp. 346-353.

Ashyk, Lori (1988). "WJW's Market Survey Finds Clevelanders Ache to Achieve." *Crain's Cleveland Business* (August 22), p. 25.

Atlas, James (1984), "Beyond Demographics," *The Atlantic Monthly* (October), pp. 49-58.

Baker, Sunny and Kim Baker (1993). *Market Mapping: How to Use Revolutionary New Software to Find, Analyze, and Keep Customers*. New York: McGraw-Hill.

Barnett, Steve (1986). "Debunking the Myth of 'Life Style.'" *Advertising Age* (August 4), p. 40.

Bayus, Barry L. and Raj Mehta (1994). "A Segmentation Model for the Targeted Marketing of Consumer Durables." Cambridge, MA: Marketing Science Institute, Technical Working Paper, pp. 94-120.

Beatty, Sally Goll (1995). "Women's Views of Their Lives Aren't Reflected by Advertisers." *The Wall Street Journal* (December 19), p. B6.

Beatty, Sharon E., Lynn R. Kahle, Pamela Homer, and Shekhar Misra (1985). "Alternative Measurement Approaches to Consumer Values: The List of Values and the Rokeach Value Survey." *Psychology and Marketing*, Vol. 2, pp. 181-220.

Beatty, Sharon E., Pamela Homer, and Lynn R. Kahle (1988). "Problems with VALS in International Marketing Research: An Example from an Application of the Empirical Mirror Technique," in Michael J. Houston (ed.). *Advances in Consumer Research XV.* Provo, UT: Association for Consumer Research.

Beckett, Sandra, Toni McNutt, and Kenneth D. Bahn (1994). "Changing Values and Lifestyle to Accommodate a Symbiotic View of Consumer Choice," in Elizabeth J. Wilson and William C. Black (eds.). *Developments in Marketing Science*, Vol. 17. Coral Gables, FL: Academy of Marketing Science, pp. 418-426.

Bellah, Robert N., Richard Madsen, William M. Sullivan, Ann Swidler, and Steven M. Tipton (1985). *Habits of the Heart: Individualism and Commitment in American Life*. New York: Harper and Row.

Berrigan, John and Carl Finkbeiner (1992). *Segmentation Marketing: New Methods for Capturing Business Markets*. New York: HarperCollins.

Berry, Dick (1988). "The Marketing Concept Revisited: It's Setting Goals, Not Making a Mad Dash for Profits." *Marketing News* (July 18), pp. 26 and 28.

Berry, Leonard L. (1979). "The Time-Buying Consumer." *Journal of Retailing,* Vol. 55 (Winter), pp. 58-69.

_____ (1990). "Market to the Perception." *American Demographics* (February), p. 32.

Berton, Lee (1989), "Innovating Means Taking Time from Same Old Grind," *The Wall Street Journal* (August 31), p. B2.

Bigness, Jon and Jonathan Dahl (1996). "Soon, Hotels Only a Boss Could Love." *The Wall Street Journal* (February 2), p. B5.

Bluedorn, Allen C., Carol Felker Kaufman, and Paul M. Lane (1992). "How Many Things do You Like to do at Once? An Introduction to Monochronic and Polychronic Time." *Academy of Management Executive*, Vol. 6, No. 4, pp. 17-26.

Bonoma, Thomas V. (1984a). "Making Your Marketing Strategy Work." *Harvard Business Review* (March/April), pp. 69-76.

_____ (1984b). *Managing Marketing: Text, Cases, and Readings*. New York: The Free Press.

_____ (1986). "Marketing Subversives." *Harvard Business Review* (November/ December), pp. 113-118.

_____ (1989). "Enough About Strategy! Let's See Some Clever Executions." *Marketing News* (February 13), pp. 10 and 14.

_____ and Benson P. Shapiro (1983). *Segmenting the Industrial Market*. Lexington, MA: Lexington Books.

Braithwaite, V. A. and H. G. Law (1985). "Structure of Human Values: Testing the Adequacy of the Rokeach Value Survey." *Journal of Personality and Social Psychology*, Vol. 49, No. 1, pp. 250-263.

Brenner, Lynn (1996). "Shareholder Targeting: Finding Investors Whose Love Will Last." *CFO* (February), pp. 57-59.

Brock, Susan A. and Lawrence Demarest (1989). "Flexible Selling: Using Type in the Sales Process," in Naomi L. Quenk (ed.). *Frontiers of Psychological Type: Proceedings of APT-VIII*. Gainesville, FL: Association for Psychological Type, pp. 112-115.

Bronner, Simon J. (1989). "Reading Consumer Culture," in Simon J. Bronner (Ed.). *Consuming Visions: Accumulation and Display of Goods in America, 1880-1920*. New York: W. W. Norton Co., pp. 13-53.

Brooksbank, Roger (1994). "The Anatomy of Marketing Positioning Strategy." *Marketing Intelligence & Planning*, Vol. 12, No. 4, pp. 10-14.

Bryant, Barbara (1986). "The Market Segmentation Cake: Survey Research Batter with Lifestyle Frosting." Paper presented at Managing Consumer Change (February 12-14), Hollywood, FL.

Burnett, John and Alan Bush (1986). "Profiling the Yuppies." *Journal of Advertising Research* (April/May), pp. 27-35.

Cadwallader, Eva H. (1980). "The Main Features of Value Experience." *Journal of Value Inquiry*, Vol. 14, pp. 229-244.

Cahill, Dennis J. (1990). "Industrializing Services: An Example of What Not to Do," in *Stayin' Alive Through '95: How to Thrive and Not Just Survive.* Chicago, IL: American Marketing Association, pp. 52-63.

_____ (1992a). "I Want a Choice, Not the 'Standard' Excuse." *Marketing News* (January 6), pp. 4 and 32.

_____ (1992b). "It's Time for Santa, the Marketing Genius. *Marketing News* (December 7), p. 4.

_____ (1992c). "The Winter Olympics as a Services Marketing Paradigm." *Services Marketing Today* (May/June), p. 4.

_____ (1993). "Why Can't They Answer a Simple Question—Like 'What Will People Buy?': A Review Essay." *Journal of Consumer Marketing,* Vol. 10, No. 2, pp. 76-79.

_____ (1994a). "A Two-Stage Model of the Search Process for Single-Family Houses: A Research Note." *Environment and Behavior,* Vol. 26, No. 1, pp. 38-48.

_____ (1994b). "A Reply to David Aaker: 'Yes You Are Talking to Yourselves, I'm Afraid.'" *ACR News,* (September), p. 11.

_____ (1995). *Squeezing a New Service into a Crowded Market.* Binghamton, NY: The Haworth Press.

_____ (1996a). *Internal Marketing: Your Company's Next Stage of Growth.* Binghamton, NY: The Haworth Press.

_____ (1996b). "What's Wrong with Service Providers? A Customer-Service Perspective." *The Journal of Customer Service in Marketing & Management,* Vol. 2, No.3.

_____ (1996c). "Why Are We Still Here, Wondering Whether What We Are Doing Is Science? A Review Essay." *Journal of Consumer Marketing,* Vol. 13, No. 3.

_____ and Robert M. Warshawsky. (1993). "The Marketing Concept: A Forgotten Aid for Marketing High-Technology Products." *Journal of Consumer Marketing,* Vol. 10, No. 1, pp. 17-22.

_____ and Sharon V. Thach (1994). "From Experience: The Marketing Concept and New High-Tech Products: Is There a Fit?" *The Journal of Product Innovation Management,* Vol. 11, No.4 (September), pp. 336-343.

Camacho, Frank E. and Diane Schmalensee (1989). "Why It's So Difficult to See the Effects of Attitudes on Sales." Paper presented at the American Marketing Association Attitude Research Conference (January 29-February 1).

Carpenter, Gregory S. and Kent Nakamoto (1989). "Consumer Preference Formation and Pioneering Advantage." *Journal of Marketing Research* (August), pp. 285-298.

_____ (1994). "Reflections on 'Consumer Preference Formation and Pioneering Advantage.'" *Journal of Marketing Research* (October), pp. 570-575.

Chavez, Catherine M. (1989). *Market Segmentation for Retail Financial Services: VALS 2 Segment Profiles and Case Studies.* Menlo Park, CA: Stanford Research Institute.

Christen, Francois G. (1987). "Richness: A Way to Evaluate Segmentation Systems." Address given at the American Marketing Association's Attitude Research Conference (April 30).

_____ and Joseph Castelli (1986). *Buying by Mail: VALS Looks at Direct Marketing.* Menlo Park, CA: Stanford Research Institute.

Claxton, Reid P. (1995). "Birth Order as a Market Segmentation Variable." *Journal of Consumer Marketing,* Vol. 12, No. 3, pp. 22-38.

Coleman, Richard P. (1983). "The Continuing Significance of Social Class to Marketing." *Journal of Consumer Research,* Vol. 10 (December), pp. 265-280.

Cooper, Lee G. (1983). "A Review of Multidimensional Scaling in Marketing Research." Working paper, the Graduate School of Management, University of California at Los Angeles, p. 10.

Crawford, John C. (1983). "The Marketing Concept–A Utopian Dream?" in John C. Rogers, III (ed.). *Developments in Marketing Science VI.* Logan, UT: Academy of Marketing Science, pp. 450-452.

Cross, James C., Thomas J. Belick, and William Rudelius (1990). "How Marketing Managers Use Market Segmentation: An Exploratory Study," in B. J. Dunlap (ed.). *Developments in Marketing Science XIII.* Cullowhee, NC: Academy of Marketing Science, pp. 532-536.

Crump, Sarah (1995). "Single Women Choosing to Build." [Cleveland] *Plain Dealer* (December 30), pp. 2-3.

Csikszentmihalyi, Mihaly, and Eugene Rochberg-Halton (1981). *The Meaning of Things: Domestic Symbols and the Self.* New York: Cambridge University Press.

Cutler, Blayne (1990). "Where Does the Free Time Go?" *American Demographics* (November), pp. 36-39.

Darian, Jean C. and Judy Cohen (1995). "Segmenting by Consumer Time Shortage." *Journal of Consumer Marketing,* Vol. 12, No. 1, pp. 32-44.

Davidow, William H. (1986). *Marketing High Technology: An Insider's View.* New York: The Free Press.

Davis, Brian and Warren A. French (1989). "Exploring Advertising Usage Segments Among the Aged." *Journal of Advertising Research,* Vol. 29 (February/March), pp. 22-29.

Day, George S. (1984). *Strategic Market Planning: The Pursuit of Competitive Advantage.* St. Paul, MN: West Publishing Company.

Demby, Emanuel (1974). "Psychographics and from Whence It Came," in William D. Wells (ed.). *Life Style and Psychographics.* Chicago, IL: American Marketing Association, pp. 11-30.

_____ (1989). "Psychographics Revisited: The Birth of a Technique." *Marketing News* (January 2), p. 21.

DeSarbo, Wayne S. and Venkatram Ramaswamy (1994). "CRISP: Customer Response-Based Iterative Segmentation Procedures for Response Modeling in Direct Marketing." Cambridge, MA: Marketing Science Institute, Technical Working Paper, pp. 94-102.

Deshpande, Rohit and Frederick C. Webster, Jr. (1989). "Organizational Culture and Marketing: Defining the Research Agenda." *Journal of Marketing* (January), pp. 3-15.

Dichter, Ernest (1986). "Whose Lifestyle Is It Anyway?" *Psychology & Marketing*, Vol. 3, pp. 151-163.

Dittmar, Helga (1992). *The Social Psychology of Material Possessions: To Have Is to Be.* New York: St. Martin's Press.

Doty, D. Harold and William H. Glick (1994). "Typologies as a Unique Form of Theory Building: Toward Improved Understanding and Modeling." *The Academy of Management Review* (April), pp. 230-251.

Douglas, Mary, and Baron Isherwood (1979). *The World of Goods.* New York: Basic Books.

Duboff, Robert S. (1992). "Marketing to Maximize Profitability." *Journal of Business Strategy*, Vol. 13 (November/December), pp. 10-13.

Egol, Len (1996). "Coke Targets Kids in Battle of the Bottle." *Direct* (January), p. 14.

Elgin, Duane. "Discovering Voluntary Simplicity." *JC Penney Forum* (November), pp. 18-20.

Engel, James F. and Roger D. Blackwell (1982). *Consumer Behavior*, 4th ed. New York: The Dryden Press.

Ensley, Elizabeth E. (1983). "Voluntary Simplicity: A Segment of Concern to Marketers?" in Patrick E. Murphy, Gene R. Laczniak, Paul F. Anderson, Russell W. Belk, O. C. Ferrell, Robert F. Lusch, Terence A. Shimp, and Charles B. Weinberg (eds.). *1983 AMA Educators' Proceedings.* Chicago: American Marketing Association, pp. 385-389.

Epstein, Gene (1995). "Myth: Americans Are Working More, Fact: More Women Are Working." *Barron's* (April 3), p. 32.

Evans, Joel R. and Barry Berman (1987). *Marketing*, 3rd. ed. New York: Macmillan Publishing Co.

Ferrell, O. C. (1985). "Implementing and Monitoring Ethics in Advertising," in Gene R. Laczniak and Patrick E. Murphy (eds.). *Marketing Ethics: Guidelines for Managers.* Lexington, MA: Lexington Books, pp. 27-40.

Fisher, James E. (1989). "Lifestyle Research in the Context of Household Economic Behavior," in Jon M. Hawes and John Thanopolos (eds.). *Developments in Marketing Science XII.* Akron, OH: Academy of Marketing Science, pp. 69-73.

Freeman, Kenneth M. (1992). "Target Marketing: The Logic of It All." *The Journal of Consumer Marketing*, Vol. 9, No. 3, pp. 15-18.

Friedlander, Frank (1975). "Emergent and Contemporary Life Styles: An Intergenerational Issue." *Human Relations*, pp. 329-347.

Freudenheim, Betty (1988). "Who Lives Here, Go-Getter or Grouch?" *The New York Times* (March 31), p. 16.

Gates, Michael (1989). "VALS Changes with the Times." *Incentive* (June), pp. 27-30 and 73.

Gilfillan, S. C. (1935). *The Sociology of Innovation.* Chicago: Follett Publishing.

Goldberg, Marvin E. (1976). "Identifying Relevant Psychographic Segments: How Specifying Product Functions Can Help." *Journal of Consumer Research*, Vol. 3 (December), pp. 163-169.

Golder, Peter N. and Gerard J. Tellis (1993). Pioneer Advantage: Marketing Logic or Marketing Legend?" *Journal of Marketing Research* (May), pp. 158-170.

Goldthwaite, Richard A. (1993). *Wealth and the Demand for Art in Italy, 1300-1600*. Baltimore: The Johns Hopkins University Press.

Gollub, James O. (1985). *Not the Same Old Story: Values Diversity Among the Aging and Effects on Consumer Behavior.* Menlo Park, CA: Stanford Research Institute.

Goodwin, Cathy and Larry Lockshin (1992). "The Solo Consumer: Unique Opportunity for the Service Marketer." *The Journal of Services Marketing*, Vol. 6, No. 3 (Summer), pp. 27-36.

Gronmo, Sigmund (1989). "Concepts of Time: Some Implications for Consumer Research," in Thomas K. Srull (ed.). *Advances in Consumer Research*, Vol. 16. Provo, UT: Association for Consumer Research, pp. 339-345.

Gross, Barbara L. and Jagdish N. Sheth (1989). "Time-Oriented Advertising: A Content Analysis of United States Magazine Advertising, 1890-1988." *Journal of Marketing*, Vol. 53 (October), pp. 76-83.

Grove, Stephen J. and Raymond P. Fisk (1989). "Impression Management in Services Marketing: A Dramaturgical Perspective," in Robert A. Giacalone and Paul Rosenfeld (eds.). *Impression Management in the Organization*. Hillsdale, NJ: Lawrence Erlbaum Associates, pp. 427-438.

_____ (1992). "The Service Experience as Theater." *Advances in Consumer Research*, XIX. Provo, UT: Association of Consumer Research, pp. 455-461.

Hallberg, Garth (1995). *All Consumers Are NOT Created Equal: The Differential Marketing Strategy for Brand Loyalty and Profits*. New York: John Wiley and Co.

Hamel, Gary and C. K. Prahalad (1994). *Competing for the Future: Breakthrough Strategies for Seizing Control of Your Industry and Creating the Markets of Tomorrow*. Boston, MA: Harvard Business School Press.

Hampden-Turner, Charles and Franklin Carlile (1986). *Lifestyle Marketing: Scenarios of Satisfaction*. Menlo Park, CA: Stanford Research Institute.

Hampton, Gerald M. and Emmett Lane. (1982). "Newspapers and the Marketing Concept: An Exploratory Study of the Attitudes of Newsroom and Management Personnel," in Vinay Kothari (ed.). *Developments in Marketing Science V*. Nagodoches, TX: Academy of Marketing Science, pp. 450-455.

Hassan, Salah S. and Lea Prevel Katsanis (1994). "Global Market Segmentation Strategies and Trends," in Salah S. Hassan and Erden A. Kaynak (eds.). *Globalization of Consumer Markets: Structures and Strategies*. Binghamton, NY: The Haworth Press, pp. 47-62.

Herche, Joel (1994). "Measuring Social Values: A Multi-item Adaptation to the List of Values (MILOV). Cambridge, MA: Marketing Science Institute, working paper, pp. 94-101.

Hirsch, James S. (1991). "Flood of Information Swamps Managers, but Some Are Finding Ways to Bail Out." *The Wall Street Journal* (August 12), pp. B1 and B5.

Hirschman, Elizabeth C. (1983). "Aesthetics, Ideologies, and the Limits of the Marketing Concept," *Journal of Marketing (Summer)*, pp. 45-55.

_____ (1985). "Primitive Aspects of Consumption in Modern American Society." *Journal of Consumer Research*, Vol. 12 (September), pp. 142-154.

Hisrich, Robert D. and Dennis J. Cahill (1995). "Buried at the Crossroads at Midnight with an Oak Stake Through Its Heart: An Entrepreneurial Replication of Ross and Staw's Extended Temporal Escalation Model." *Family Business Review*, Vol. 8 (Spring), pp. 41-54.

Holbrook, Morris B. (1987). "O, Consumer, How You've Changed: Some Radical Reflections on the Roots of Consumption," in A. Fuat Firat, Nikhilesh Dholakia, and Richard P. Bagozzi (eds.). *Philosophical and Radical Thought in Marketing.* Lexington, MA: Lexington Book, pp. 156-177.

_____ (1995). *Consumer Research: Introspective Essays on the Study of Consumption.* Thousand Oaks, CA: SAGE Publications.

Holt, Douglas B. (1995). "How Consumers Consume: A Typology of Consumption Practices." *Journal of Consumer Research*, Vol. 22 (June), pp. 1-16.

Horne, David A., John P. McDonald, and David L. Williams. (1986). "Consumer Perception of Service Dimensions: Implications for Marketing Strategy," in M. Venkatesan, Diane M. Schmalensee, and Claudia Marshall, (eds.). *Creativity in Services Marketing: What's New, What Works, What's Developing.* Chicago: American Marketing Association, pp. 35-39.

Hortman, Sandra McCurley, Arthur W. Allaway, J. Barry Mason, and John Rays (1990). "Multisegment Analysis of Supermarket Patronage." *Journal of Business Research*, Vol. 21, pp. 209-223.

Hymowitz, Carol (1991). "Trading Fat Paychecks for Free Time." *The Wall Street Journal* (August 5), p. B1.

Jackson, Barbara Bund (1985). *Winning & Keeping Industrial Customers: The Dynamics of Customer Relationships.* Lexington, MA: Lexington Books.

Jellinek, Mariann and Claudia Bird Schoonhoven (1994). *The Innovation Marathon: Lessons from High-Technology Firms.* San Francisco: Jossey-Bass Publishers.

Johnson, KerenAnn and Scott D. Roberts (1992). "Incompletely-Launched and Returning Young Adults: Social Change, Consumption, and Family Environment," in Robert P. Leone and V. Kumar (eds.). *1992 AMA Educators' Proceedings.* Chicago, IL: American Marketing Association, pp. 249-254.

Kahle, Lynn R. (ed.). (1983). *Social Values and Social Change: Adaptation to Life in America.* New York: Praeger.

_____ (1986). "The Nine Nations of North America and the Value Basis of Geographic Segmentation." *Journal of Marketing*, Vol. 50 (April), pp. 37-47.

_____, Sharon E. Beatty, and Pamela Homer (1986). "Alternative Measurement Approaches to Consumer Values: The List of Values (LOV) and Values and

Life Style (VALS)." *Journal of Consumer Research*, Vol. 13 (December), pp. 405-409.

Kahle, Lynn R. and Patricia Kennedy (1988). "Using the List of Values (LOV) to Understand Consumers." *Journal of Consumer Marketing*, Vol. 6 (Summer), pp. 5-12.

Kahle, Lynn R., Basil Poulos, and Ajay Sukhdial (1988). "Changes in Social Values in the United States During the Past Decade." *Journal of Advertising Research*, Vol. 28 (February/March), pp. 35-41.

Kamakura, Wagner A. and Jose Afonso Mazzon (1991). "Value Segmentation: A Model for the Measurement of Values and Value Systems." *Journal of Consumer Research*, Vol. 18 (September), pp. 208-218.

Kamakura, Wagner A. and Thomas P. Novak (1992). "Value-System Segmentation: Exploring the Meaning of LOV." *Journal of Consumer Research*, Vol. 19 (June), pp. 119-132.

Kassarjian, Harold H. (1971). "Personality and Consumer Behavior: A Review." *Journal of Marketing Research*, Vol. 8 (November), pp. 409-418.

Katzenstein, Herbert and William S. Sachs (1986). *Direct Marketing*. Columbus, OH: Charles E. Merrill Publishing Co.

Kaufman, Carol Felker (1995). "Shop 'Til You Drop: Tales from a Physically Challenged Shopper." *Journal of Consumer Marketing*, Vol. 12, No. 3, pp. 39-55.

_____ and Paul M. Lane (n.d.,a). "Bridging the Time-Use Measurement Gap: Insights, Issues, and Problems from Five Major Time-Use Studies." Unpublished working paper.

_____ (n.d.,b). "Standard Clocks, Non-Standard People: Research Limitations of the Fixed-Resource Approach to Time." Unpublished working paper.

Kelman, Herbert C. (1980). "The Role of Action in Attitude Change," in Monte M. Page (ed.). *Beliefs, Attitudes, and Values: Nebraska Symposium on Motivation, 1979*. Lincoln, NB: University of Nebraska Press, pp. 117-194.

Kerin, Roger A., P. Rajan Varadarajan, and Robert A. Peterson (1992). "First-Mover Advantage: A Synthesis, Conceptual Framework and Research Propositions." *Journal of Marketing* (October), pp. 33-52.

Kilmann, Ralph H., Mary J. Saxton, and Roy Serpa (1986). "Issues in Understanding and Changing Culture." *California Management Review*, pp. 87-109.

Kimball, Robert J. (1982). *Media Usage by the VALS Types*. Menlo Park, CA: Stanford Research Institute.

Kohli, Chiranjeev S. and Lance Leuthesser. (1993). "Product Positioning: A Comparison of Perceptual Mapping Techniques." *The Journal of Product & Brand Management*, Vol. 2, No. 4, pp. 10-19.

Kowalysko, Ihor A. (n.d.,a). "Analyzing Two-Dimensional MDPREF Configurations Using Non-Parametric Statistics." Working paper of Wyse Advertising Co., Cleveland, OH.

_____ (n.d.,b). "MDPREF–A Tool for Mapping of Perceptual Data." Working paper of Wyse Advertising Co., Cleveland, OH.

Lai, Albert Wenben (1995). "Consumer Values, Product Benefits and Customer Value: A Consumption Behavior Approach," in Frank R. Kardes and Mita Sujan (eds.). *Advances in Consumer Research*, Vol. 22. Provo, UT: Association for Consumer Research, pp. 381-388.

Lane, Paul M. And Carol J. Kaufman (n.d.,a). "Standardizing Time Across Cultures." Unpublished working paper.

_____ (n.d.,b). "Time Waves: Mental and Physical Intensity Over Clock Time." Unpublished working paper.

Lastovicka, John L. (1982). "On the Validation of Lifestyle Traits: A Review and Illustration." *Journal of Marketing Research* (February), pp. 126-138.

Lavin, Marilyn (1993). "Husband-dominant, Wife-dominant, Joint: A Shopping Typology for Baby Boom Couples." *The Journal of Consumer Marketing*, Vol. 10, No. 3, pp. 33-42.

Lawrence, Gordon (1982). *People Types and Tiger Stripes: A Practical Guide to Learning Styles, 2nd ed.* Palo Alto, CA: Consulting Psychologists Press.

Lee, Keun S. and Paul J. Hensel (1990). "Conceptual and Methodological Issues in Contemporary Values Research in Consumer Behavior: A Critical Analysis," in B. J. Dunlap (ed.). *Developments in Marketing Science XIII*. Cullowhee, NC: Academy of Marketing Science, pp. 30-34.

Leonard-Barton, Dorothy (1981). "Voluntary Simplicity Lifestyles and Energy Conservation." *Journal of Consumer Research* (December), pp. 243-242.

Lesser, Jack A. and Marie Adele Hughes (1986). "The Generalizability of Psychographic Market Segments Across Geographic Locations." *Journal of Marketing*, (January), pp. 18-27.

Lincoln, Yvonna S. (1985). *Organizational Theory and Inquiry: The Paradigm Revolution*. Beverly Hills, CA: SAGE Publications.

Lofland, Laurie and Nabil Y. Razzouk (1992). "Revisiting the Family Life Cycle: Modifications and Implications," in Victoria L. Crittenden (ed.). *Developments in Marketing Science*, Vol. 15. Chesnut Hill, MA: Academy of Marketing Science, pp. 43-47.

Longfellow, Timothy A. and Kevin G. Celuch (1993). "Segmenting Customers by Their Degree of Service Involvement," in David W. Cravens and Peter R. Dickson (eds.). *1993 AMA Educators' Proceedings*. Chicago, IL: American Marketing Association, pp. 390-396.

Loyalty Marketing: The Wave of the Future (1986). New York: The Russell D. Levitt Co.

Lublin, Joann S. (1995). "Family Values: Some Adult Daughters of 'Supermoms' Plan to Take Another Path." *The Wall Street Journal* (December 28), pp. A1 and A2.

MacEvoy, Bruce H. (1989). *Technical Development of the VALS 2 System*. Menlo Park, CA: Stanford Research Institute.

Maher, Philip (1983). "Psychographics and Corporate Advertising: Powerful Techniques Are Slowly Taking Hold." *Industrial Marketing* (February), pp. 64, 68, and 71.

Martellaro, John (1996). "More People Opting for a Simpler Lifestyle." [Cleveland] *Plain Dealer* (February 10), pp. 1E and 4E.

Martin, Dawne and Kenneth A. Hunt (1987). "Toward an Integrative Model of Organizational Buying Behavior," in Russell W. Belk et al. (eds.) *Marketing Theory: 1987 AMA Winter Educators Conference*. Chicago, IL: American Marketing Association, pp. 290-294.

Martin, Maria (1989). *Characteristics of the VALS 2 Segments: Demographics, Attitudes, Consumption Patterns, Activities, and Media Use*. Menlo Park, CA: Stanford Research Institute.

Mason, Roger (1992). "Modeling the Demand for Status Goods," in Floyd Rudmin and Marsha Richins (eds.). *Meaning, Measure, and Morality of Materialism*. Provo, UT: Association for Consumer Research, pp. 88-91.

Mather, John H. (1985). "No Reason to Fear 'Frightening' Reality of VALS." *Marketing News* (September 13), p. 15.

McBride, Michael H. and Carolyn G. Cline. "Segmenting Audiences by Type and Temperament in a Marketing Campaign," in Naomi L. Quenk (ed.) *Frontiers of Psychological Type: Proceedings of APT-VIII*. Gainesville, FL: Association for Psychological Type, pp. 123-126.

McCracken, Grant (1988). *Culture and Consumption: New Approaches to the Symbolic Character of Consumer Goods and Activities*. Bloomington, IN: Indiana University Press.

McDaid, Gerald P., Mary H. McCaulley, and Richard I. Kainz (1986). *Myers-Briggs Type Indicator Atlas of Type Tables*. Palo Alto, CA: Consulting Psychologists Press.

McIntyre, Roger P., Reid P. Claxton, and David B. Jones (1994). "Empirical Relationships Between Cognitive Style and LOV: Implications for Values and Value Systems," in Christ T. Allen and Deborah Roedder John (eds.). *Advances in Consumer Research*, Vol. 21. Provo, UT: Association for Consumer Research, pp. 141-146.

McKitterick, John B. (1957). "What Is the Marketing Management Concept?" in Frank M. Bass (ed.). *The Frontiers of Marketing Thought and Action*. Chicago: American Marketing Association, pp. 71-82.

McNeal, James U. (1987). *Children as Consumers: Insights and Implications*. Lexington, MA: Lexington Books.

Merenski, J. Paul (1981). "Psychographics: Valid by Definition and Reliable by Technique," in Venkatakrishna V. Bellur (ed.). *Developments in Marketing Science*, Vol. IV. Muncie, IN: Academy of Marketing Science, pp. 161-166.

Meyer, Philip (1983). "The ABCs of Psychographics." *American Demographics*.

Michman, Ronald D. (1991). *Lifestyle Market Segmentation*. New York: Praeger.

Miller, Cyndee (1996). "Boomers Come of Age: Marketers Now Likely to view Mature Market in New Light." *Marketing News*, Vol. 30 (January 15), pp. 1 and 6.

Miller, Michael W. (1987). "At Many Firms, Employees Speak a Language That's All Their Own." *The Wall Street Journal*, December 29, p. 15.

Miller, William C. (1987). *Fostering Creativity: The VALS Perspective.* Menlo Park, CA: Stanford Research Institute.

Mills, Michael K. (1981). "Market Segmentation: A New Look at an Old Topic," in Venkatakrishna V. Bellur (ed.). *Developments in Marketing Science,* Vol. IV. Muncie, IN: Academy of Marketing Science, pp. 167-170.

Mills, Stephen J. (1988). *Participatory Health: VALS and Consumer Health Attitudes and Behavior.* Menlo Park, CA: Stanford Research Institute.

Mitchell, Arnold (1981a). *Proximities of the VALS Types.* Menlo Park, CA: Stanford Research Institute.

_____ (1981b). *The VALS Typology: Summary 1981.* Menlo Park, CA: Stanford Research Institute.

_____ (1981c). *Flows in the VALS Typology.* Menlo Park, CA: Stanford Research Institute.

_____ (1983a). *The Nine American Lifestyles: Who We Are and Where We're Going.* New York: Warner Books.

_____ (1983b). *Types of Belongers.* Menlo Park, CA: Stanford Research Institute.

_____ (1983c). *Types of Achievers.* Menlo Park, CA: Stanford Research Institute.

_____ (1983d). *Regional and Other Distributions of the VALS Types.* Menlo Park, CA: Stanford Research Institute.

_____ (1984). *The Marrieds: Patterns, Attitudes, and Decision Making of the VALS Marrieds.* Menlo Park, CA: Stanford Research Institute.

_____ (1985). *Inner Needs and the Marketplace: An Exploratory Look.* Menlo Park, CA: Stanford Research Institute.

_____ and Robert J. Kimball (1984). *Values and the Purchase Decision.* Menlo Park, CA: Stanford Research Institute.

Mitchell, Vincent-Wayne (1994a). "How to Identify Psychographic Segments: Part 1." *Marketing Intelligence & Planning,* Vol. 12, No. 7, pp. 4-10.

_____ (1994b). "How To Identify Psychographic Segments: Part 2." *Marketing Intelligence & Planning,* Vol. 12, No. 7, pp. 11-17.

Miyazaki, Anthony D. (1993). "How Many Shopping Days Until Christmas? A Preliminary Investigation of Time Pressures, Deadlines, and Planning Levels on Holiday Gift Purchases," in Leigh McAlister and Michael L. Rothschild (eds.). *Advances in Consumer Research,* Vol. 20. Provo, UT: Association for Consumer Research, pp. 331-335.

"Mom's Munching Habits," (1995). *Advertising Age* (May 1), p. 3.

Morgan, Fred W., Jr., Richard C. Becherer, and Lawrence M. Richard (1979). "Product Trial and Product Usage: Bases for a Strategic Segmentation Framework," in Howard S. Gitlow and Edward W. Wheatley (eds.). *Developments in Marketing Science,* Vol. II. Miami, FL: Academy of Marketing Science, pp. 305-307.

Moschis, George (1992). "Gerontographics: A Scientific Approach to Analyzing and Targeting the Mature Market." *The Journal of Services Marketing,* Vol. 6, No. 3 (Summer), pp. 17-26.

_____ (1993). "Gerontographics: A Scientific Approach to Analyzing and Targeting the Mature Market." *The Journal of Consumer Marketing*, Vol. 10, No. 3, pp. 43-53.

Muzyka, Daniel P., Vicky L. Crittenden, and William F. Crittenden (1986). "Market Segmentation in Industrial Marketing Strategy," in Terence Shimp, et al. (eds.). *1986 AMA Educators' Proceedings*. Chicago, IL: American Marketing Association, pp. 315-320.

Myers, Isabel Briggs, with Peter B. Myers (1980). *Gifts Differing*. Palo Alto, CA: Consulting Psychologists Press.

Myers, Isabel Briggs and Mary H. McCaulley (1985). *Manual: A Guide to the Development and Use of the Myers-Briggs Type Indicator*. Palo Alto, CA: Consulting Psychologists Press.

Nasar, Jack L. (1988a). "Architectural Symbolism: A Study of House-Style Meanings," Paper prepared for the Environmental Design Research Association Conference, Pomona, CA.

_____ (1988b). Letter to Dennis J. Cahill.

_____ (1989). "Symbolic Meanings of House Styles." *Environment and Behavior*, Vol. 21, No. 3 (May), pp. 235-257.

National Market Measures (1985). Research Report on Habitat's Advertising Focus Group.

_____ (1988). Qualitative Research Results for Home Characterizations.

Neidell, Lester A. (1983). *Strategic Marketing Management: An Integrated Approach*. Tulsa, OK: PennWell Books.

Newhouse News Service (1991). "You May be Tired but Study Says You Work Less, Play More." [Cleveland] *Plain Dealer* (November 3), p. 3-A.

Nicosia, Francesco M. and Robert N. Mayer (1976). "Toward a Sociology of Consumption." *Journal of Consumer Research*, Vol. 3 (September), pp. 65-75.

Novak, Thomas P. and Bruce MacEvoy (1990). "On Comparing Alternative Segmentation Schemes: The List of Values (LOV) and Values and Life Styles (VALS)." *Journal of Consumer Research*, Vol. 17 (June), pp. 105-109.

Novak, Thomas P., Jan de Leeuw, and Bruce MacEvoy (1992). "Richness Curves for Evaluating Market Segmentation." *Journal of Marketing Research*, Vol. 29 (May), pp. 251-267.

O'Boyle, Thomas F. (1991). "Fast-Track Kids Exhaust Their Parents." *The Wall Street Journal* (August 7), pp. B1 and B8.

Ochs, Mal (1988). *Spending Media Dollars Smarter: The VALS Approach*. Menlo Park, CA: Stanford Research Institute.

Ogilvy, James (1985). *The Experience Industry*. Menlo Park, CA: Stanford Research Institute.

_____ (1986). "The Experience Industry." *American Demographics* (December), pp. 26-29 and 59.

O'Malley, Lisa, Maurice Patterson, and Martin Evans (1995). "Retailing Applications of Geodemographics: A Preliminary Investigation." *Marketing Intelligence & Planning*, Vol. 13, No. 2, pp. 29-35.

Ouchi, William G. and Alan L Wilkins (1985). "Organizational Culture," *Annual Review of Sociology*, XI. Palo Alto, CA: Annual Reviews, Inc., pp. 457-483.

Pacanowsky, Michael E. and Nick O'Donnell-Trujillo (1983). "Organizational Communication as Cultural Performance." *Communication Monographs (June)*, pp. 126-147.

Page, Christine (1992). "A History of Conspicuous Consumption," in Floyd Rudmin and Marsha Richins (eds.). *Meaning, Measure, and Morality of Materialism*. Provo, UT: Association for Consumer Research, pp. 82-87.

Page-Wood, Esther S., Carol J. Kaufman, and Paul M. Lane (1990). "The Art of Time," in B. J. Dunlap (ed.) *Developments in Marketing Science*, Vol. 13. Cullowhee, NC: Academy of Marketing Science, pp. 56-61.

Pearson, Andrail E. (1988). "Tough-Minded Ways to Get Innovative," *Harvard Business Review (May/June)*, pp. 99-106.

Peppers, Don and Marsha Rogers (1993). *The One-to-One Future: Building Relationships One Customer at a Time*. New York: Currency-Doubleday.

Perkins, W. Steven and Thomas J. Reynolds (1988). "The Explanatory Power of Values in Preference Judgements: Validation of the Means-End Perspective," in Michael J. Houston (ed.). *Advances in Consumer Research*, XV. Provo, UT: Association for Consumer Research, pp. 122-126.

Piirto, Rebecca (1990). "Measuring Minds in the 1990s." *American Demographics* (December), pp. 30-35.

_____ (1991). *Beyond Mind Games: The Marketing Power of Psychographics*. Ithaca, NY: American Demographics Books.

Pitts, Robert E. Jr. and Arch G. Woodside (1984). *Personal Values and Consumer Psychology*. Lexington, MA: Lexington Books.

Ploss, Kathryn (1987). *The VALS Types, 1987: Demographics, Attitudes, Consumption Patterns, Activities, and Media Usage*. Menlo Park, CA: SRI, International.

Plummer, Joseph T. (1974). "The Concept and Application of Life Style Segmentation." *Journal of Marketing*, Vol. 38 (January), pp. 33-37.

Pollay, Richard W. (1984). "The Identification and Distribution of Values Manifest in Print Advertising, 1900-1980," in Robert E. Pitts, Jr. and Arch G. Woodside (eds.). *Personal Values and Consumer Psychology*. Lexington, MA: Lexington Books, pp. 111-125.

_____, Jung S. Lee, and David Carter-Whitney (1992). "Separate, but Not Equal: Racial Segmentation in Cigarette Advertising." *Journal of Advertising*, Vol. 21 (March), pp. 45-57.

Pollay, Richard W. and Banwari Mittal (1993). "Here's the Beef: Factors, Determinants, and Segments in Consumer Criticisms of Advertising." *Journal of Marketing*, Vol. 57 (July), pp. 99-114.

Porter, Michael E. (1985). *Competitive Advantage: Creating and Sustaining Superior Performance*. New York: The Free Press.

Prakash, Ved. and J. Michael Munson (1985). "Values, Expectations from the Marketing System and Product Expectations." *Psychology & Marketing*, Vol. 2 (Winter), pp. 279-296.

Rafiq, Mohammed and Pervaiz K. Ahmed (1993). "The Scope of Internal Marketing: Defining the Boundary Between Marketing and Human Resource Management." *Journal of Marketing Management*, Vol. 9, pp. 219-232.

Rangan, V. Kasturi, Rowland T. Moriarty, and Gordon S. Swartz (1992). "Segmenting Customers in Mature Industrial Markets." *Journal of Marketing*, Vol. 56 (October), pp. 72-82.

Rapoport, Amos (1982). *The Meaning of the Built Environment: A Nonverbal Communication Approach*. Beverly Hills, CA: Sage Publications.

Rescher, Nicholas (1967). "The Study of Value Change." *Journal of Value Inquiry*, Vol. 1, pp. 12-23.

Riche, Martha Farnsworth (1989). Psychographics for the 1990s." *American Demographics* (July), pp. 24-26, 30-31, and 53.

Ries, Al (1992). "The Discipline of the Narrow Focus." *Journal of Business Strategy*, Vol. 13 (November/December), pp. 3-9.

Riesman, David, with Nathan Glazer and Reuel Denney (1950/1961). *The Lonely Crowd*. New Haven, CT: Yale University Press.

Rigdon, Joan E. (1991). "Managers Who Switch Coasts Must Adapt to Different Approaches to Use of Time." *The Wall Street Journal* (August 14), pp. B1 and B6.

Roberts, Kristin and Peter Rupert (1995). "The Myth of the Overworked American." *Economic Commentary of the Federal Reserve Bank of Cleveland* (January 15).

Roberts, Scott D., Patricia K. Voli, and KerenAnn Johnson (1992). "Beyond the Family Life Cycle: An Inventory of Variables for Defining the Family as a Consumption Unit," in Victoria L. Crittenden (ed.). *Developments in Marketing Science*, Vol. 15. Chesnut Hill, MA: Academy of Marketing Science, pp. 71-75.

Robertson, Thomas S. and Yoram Wind (1980). "Organizational Psychographics and Innovativeness." *Journal of Consumer Research*, Vol. 7 (June), pp. 24-31.

Robinson, John P. (1989). "Time's Up." *American Demographics*, (July) pp. 33-35.

_____ (1990). "The Time Squeeze." *American Demographics* (February), pp. 30-33.

Robinson, William T. (1988). "Sources of Market Pioneer Advantages: The Case of Industrial Goods Industries." *Journal of Marketing Research* (February), pp. 87-94.

Rogers, Everett M. (1983). *Diffusion of Innovations*, 3rd. edition. New York: The Free Press.

Rogers, John C., Mark Slama, and Terrell G. Williams (1983). "An Exploratory Study of Luscher Color Test Predicted Personality Types and Psychographic Shopping Profiles," in Patrick E. Murphy, Gene R. Laczniak, Paul F. Anderson, Russell W. Belk, O. C. Ferrell, Robert F. Lusch, Terence A. Shimp, and Charles B. Weinberg (eds.). *1983 AMA Educators' Proceedings*. Chicago, IL: American Marketing Association, pp. 30-34.

Rokeach, Milton (1968). *Beliefs, Attitudes, and Values: A Theory of Organization and Change*. San Francisco: Jossey-Bass, Inc.

_____ (1968-1969). "The Role of Values in Public Opinion Research." *Public Opinion Quarterly*, (Winter), pp. 547-559.

_____ (1979). "From Individual to Institutional Values: With Special Reference to the Values of Science," in Milton Rokeach (ed.). *Understanding Human Values: Individual and Societal*. New York: The Free Press, pp. 47-70.

Rook, Dennis W. (1985). "The Ritual Dimension of Consumer Behavior." *Journal of Consumer Research*, Vol. 12 (December), pp. 251-264.

Sadalla, Edward K., Beth Vershure, and Jeffrey Burroughs (1987). "Identity Symbolism in Housing." *Environment and Behavior*, Vol. 19, No. 5 (September), pp. 569-587.

Saffold, Guy S. (1988). "Culture Traits, Strength, and Organizational Performance: Moving Beyond 'Strong' Culture," *Academy of Management Review*, pp. 546-558.

Saporito, Bill (1995). "What's for Dinner? The Battle for Stomach Share." *Fortune* (May 15), pp. 50-52 and cf.

Schaninger, Charles M. and William D. Danko (1993). "A Conceptual and Empirical Comparison of Alternative Household Life Cycle Models." *Journal of Consumer Research*, Vol. 19 (March), pp. 580-594.

Schein, Edgar H. (1985). *Organizational Culture and Leadership: A Dynamic View*. San Francisco: Josscy-Bass Inc.

Schmalensee, Richard and Jacques-Francois Thisse (1986). "Perceptual Maps and the Optimal Location of New Products." Cambridge, MA: Marketing Science Institute, Technical Working Paper, pp. 86-103.

Schnaars, Steven P. (1991). *Marketing Strategy: A Customer-Driven Approach*. New York: The Free Press.

_____ (1994). *Managing Imitation Strategies*. New York: The Free Press.

Schultz, Don (1994). "What Advertisers and Consumers Wanted in the Past, They Are Not Going to Want in the Future." *Link* (June), p. 44.

Schwartz, Peter and James Ogilvy (1979). *The Emergent Paradigm: Changing Patterns of Thought and Belief*. Menlo Park, CA: Stanford Research Institute.

Shapiro, Benson P. and Thomas V. Bonoma (1983). "How to Segment Industrial Markets." *Harvard Business Review* (May/June), pp. 104-110.

Sherif, Carolyn Wood. (1980). "Social Values, Attitudes, and Involvement of the Self," in Monte M. Page (ed.). *Beliefs, Attitudes, and Values: Nebraska Symposium on Motivation, 1979*. Lincoln, NB: University of Nebraska Press, pp. 1-64.

Shugan, Steven M. (1987). "Establishing Brand Positioning Maps Using Supermarket Scanning Data." *Journal of Marketing Research* (February), pp. 1-18.

Sisodia, Rajendra S. (1993). "The 'Ideal' Brokerage Firm: Revealed Structure and Symmetries in the Institutional Equity Services Market." *Journal of Professional Services Marketing*, Vol. 10, No. 1, pp. 119-145.

Skidmore, Sarita A. and Ronald H. Pyszka (1986). *Travel and Values*. Menlo Park, CA: Stanford Research Institute.

Smircich, Linda (1983). "Concepts of Culture and Organizational Analysis," *Administrative Science Quarterly*, pp. 339-358.

Spates, James L. (1983). "The Sociology of Values." *Annual Review of Sociology*, IX. Palo Alto, CA: Annual Reviews Inc., pp. 27-49.

SRI International (1983). *American Portrait*. Menlo Park, CA: Stanford Research International.

_____ (1989). *Consumer Portraits*. Menlo Park, CA: Stanford Research International.

Stacey, Ralph D. (1992). *Managing the Unknowable: Strategic Boundaries Between Order and Chaos in Organizations*. San Francisco: Jossey-Bass Publishers.

Staw, Barry M. (1976). "Knee Deep in the Big Muddy: A Study of Escalating Commitment to a Chosen Course of Action," *Organizational Behavior and Human Performance*, p. 27.

Staw, Barry M. and Jerry Ross (1987a). "Understanding Escalation Situations: Antecedents, Prototypes, and Solutions," in L. L. Cummings and Barry M. Staw (eds.) *Research in Organizational Behavior*. Greenwich, CT: JAI Press.

_____ (1987b). "Knowing When to Pull the Plug," *Harvard Business Review* (March/April), pp. 68-74.

Steinhart, Peter (1985). "Simplicity." *Audubon* (November), pp. 6, 8-9.

Tilton, James (1988). Personal conversation with author.

Tinney, Cathie H. (1989). "Life Begins When the Kids Leave Home and the Dog Dies–But That's Where the Family Life Cycle Ends," in Jon M. Hawes and John Thanopolos (eds.). *Developments in Marketing Science*, XII. Akron, OH: Academy of Marketing Science, pp. 59-63.

Townsend, Bickley (1985). "Psychographic Glitter and Gold." *American Demographics* (November).

Valeriano, Lourdes Lee (1991). "Executives Find They're Always on Call as Computer, Fax Supersede Time Zones." *The Wall Street Journal* (August 8), pp. B1 and B3.

Values and Lifestyles Program (1989). *VALS 2: Consumer Segmentation for the 1990s*. Menlo Park, CA: Stanford Research Institute.

Verba, Steven M. and Dennis J. Cahill (1993). "Interactivity: The Successful Semiotics of a Product Failure," in *Proceedings of the Third Biennial High Technology Management Conference*, University of Colorado. Boulder, CO: University of Colorado, pp. 377-383.

Vinson, Donald E. and J. Michael Munson (1976). "Personal Values: An Approach to Market Segmentation," in Kenneth L. Bernhardt (ed.). *Marketing: 1877-1976 and Beyond*. Chicago, IL: American Marketing Association, pp. 313-317.

Waldrop, Judith (1989). "Inside America's Households." *American Demographics* (March), pp. 20-27.

The Wall Street Journal (1990a). *The American Way of Buying*. New York: Dow Jones & Co.

_____ (1990b). *What the Customer Wants: The Wall Street Journal's Guide to Marketing in the 1990's*. New York Dow Jones & Co.

Walling, Victor C., Jr. (1984). *VALS and Innovation*. Menlo Park, CA: Stanford Research Institute.

Wang, Zhengyuan and C. P. Rao (1995). "Personal Values and Shopping Behavior: A Structural Equation Test of the RVS in China," in Frank R. Kardes and Mita Sujan (eds.). *Advances in Consumer Research*, Vol. 22. Provo, UT: Association for Consumer Research, pp. 373-380.

Warrick, Brooke H. (1984). *Intellectual and Emotional Styles of the VALS Types.* Menlo Park, CA: SRI International, Inc.

Wasmer, D.J. and Gordon C. Bruner II (1991). "Using Organizational Culture to Design Internal Marketing Strategies." *The Journal of Services Marketing,* Vol. 5, No. 1, (Winter), pp. 35-46.

Wasson, Jeanie L. (1987). "Psychographics: An Aid to Demographics." *Adweek's Marketing Week* (September 11), p. 48.

Weinstein, Art (1987). *Market Segmentation: Using Niche Marketing to Exploit New Markets.* Chicago, IL: Probus Publishing Co.

_____ (1994). *Market Segmentation: Using Demographics, Psychographics and Other Niche Marketing Techniques to Predict Customer Behavior,* revised edition. Chicago, IL: Probus Publishing Co.

Weiss, Michael J. (1988). *The Clustering of America.* New York Harper & Row.

_____ (1994). *Latitudes and Attitudes: An Atlas of American Tastes, Trends, Politics, and Passions from Abilene, Texas, to Zanesville, Ohio.* Boston: Little, Brown and Company.

Wells, William D. (1975). "Psychographics: A Critical Review." *Journal of Marketing Research*, Vol. 12 (May), pp. 196-213.

_____ and Geri Moore (1989). "I Can Hear It, Coggins . . . America's Values Are Shifting Again." Paper Presented at the American Marketing Association Attitude Research Conference, January 29-February 1.

Wilkie, William L. and Joel B. Cohen (1977). "An Overview of Market Segmentation: Behavioral Concepts and Research Approaches." Cambridge, MA: Marketing Science Institute, working paper, pp. 77-105.

Williams, Alvin J. and A. Ben Oumlil (1983). "Organizational Psychographics: Implications for Industrial Marketing," in John C. Rogers, III (ed.). *Developments in Marketing Science*, Vol. 6. Logan, UT: Academy of Marketing Science, p. 198.

Williams, Robin M., Jr. (1967). "Individual and Group Values." *The Annals of the American Academy of Political and Social Science*, No. 371 (May), pp. 20-37.

_____ (1979). "Change and Stability in Values and Value Systems: A Sociological Perspective," in Milton Rokeach (ed.). *Understanding Human Values: Individual and Societal.* New York: The Free Press, pp. 15-46.

Wind, Yoram and Robert J. Thomas (1994). "Segmenting Industrial Markets," in Arch G. Woodside (ed.). *Advances in Business Marketing and Purchasing*, Vol. 6. Greenwich, CT: JAI Press, Inc., pp. 59-82.

Winters, Lewis C. (1989). "New Technologies: SRI Announces VALS 2." *Marketing Research: A Magazine of Management & Applications* (June), pp. 67-69.

WJW-TV8 (1988). "Profiles for Advertising to Consumers Effectively." Cleveland, OH: Marshall Marketing and Communications, Inc.

Wolfe, David B. (1992). "The Key to Marketing to Older Consumers." *Journal of Business Strategy*, Vol. 13 (November/December), pp. 14-18.

Yavitz, Boris and William H. Newman (1982). *Strategy in Action: The Execution, Politics, and Payoff of Business Planning*. New York: The Free Press.

Yeakley, Flavil R., Jr. (1982). "Communication Style Preferences and Adjustments as an Approach for Studying Effects of Similarity in Psychological Type." *Research in Psychological Type*, Vol. 5, pp. 30-48.

_____ (1983). "Implications of Communication Style Research for Psychological Type Theory." *Research in Psychological Type*, Vol. 6, pp. 5-23.

Zenzen, Michael J. and Louis Z. Hammer (1978). "Value Measurement and Existential Wholeness: A Critique of the Rokeachean Approach to Value Research." *The Journal of Value Inquiry*, Vol. 12 (Spring), pp. 142-156.

Zerubavel, Eviatar (1987). "The Language of Time: Towards a Semiotics of Temporality." *The Sociological Quarterly*, Vol. 28, No. 3, pp. 343-356.

Ziff, Ruth (1974). "The Rise of Psychographics in the Development of Advertising Strategy and Copy," in William D. Wells (ed.). *Life Style and Psychographics*. Chicago, IL: American Marketing Association, pp. 127-155.

Index